Driving in Europe 101

CURLEY BOWMAN

A Pig Penned Publication • Maitland, Florida, USA

Graphics: Robert Smith, Jr.

Layout: Jessica Kiela

International Standard Book Number: 1-59975-489-4

Library of Congress Control Number: 2006903542

Published by: A Pig Penned Publication, Maitland, Florida, USA

To my wife Jan for sharing my dreams.

To our parents for gifting us our adventurous nature.

To our sons, Chad and Joey, who instilled the desire to get the heck out of town.

And a special thanks to all those gracious people who responded to my plea for help with translations, laws and customs of their respective countries. People from police departments, embassies, travel bureaus and hotels, students, teachers, and just plain folk from around the world made this book possible.

Life is not measured by how many breaths you take;
it is measured by those moments that take your breath away.
(Unknown)

TABLE OF CONTENTS

SECTION I
THE BASICS

1 INTRODUCTION

It is the journey that is important, not the destination.
(Unknown)

WHY IN A CAR

I cannot pin down the author of this thought but, without question, it summarizes why you may want to consider a driving vacation through Europe. Your pace is your own. You will see sights, meet people, taste foods, and sleep in small villages you would have never encountered on a high-speed, organized tour. I am not a travel agent, nor do I work for a rental car agency or a hotel chain, and nor am I connected to the travel industry in any way. The intent of this book is not to sell you on the idea of driving through Belgium, Germany or Austria.[1] This is not a travel guide. Once you have decided to embark upon a driving vacation through Europe, you will find the information in the following pages most valuable. They will make your trip safer and possibly save you a few bucks. Hopefully, these pages will also add dimensions to your travel experience you would not have otherwise enjoyed.

One of the most interesting things about traveling through parts of Europe is that castles seem to magically appear upon hilltops. They are everywhere. Some are free to visit; others may be toured for a modest fee. On a bus – not an option. See a lonely gravel road trailing into the mountains that you would like to explore? In a train – no chance. See a charming sidewalk café attached to a building built 500 years ago where you would like to eat or simply sip a cup of coffee? With a group – take a vote.

Still not decided? Need another reason? Do you dream of escaping the summer temperatures that jump to the high 90's daily? Pull your son's globe off the shelf. That's that big-ball-thingy you purchased thinking your son would absorb geographic knowledge by osmosis if you simply put it by his bed. Put your finger in the middle of Europe and drag it around to the western hemisphere. This should take you across Greenland and put you somewhere on the northern side of Ontario. Voilá! (Pronounced: vwä-´lä, a word the French say before or after every phrase. Depending where you are from, it generally translates to "Ah-Ha" or "Tah-Da.") Now you understand why the temperatures are generally much cooler in Europe than Anywhere, USA.

---

[1] Actually, two of my "intents" are: 1) To make a few bucks through the sale of this book; and 2) To improve the reputation of those crazy American drivers in the countries where I plan to drive in the future.

CAUTION: If you cannot follow the previous instructions pertaining to the globe, you may want to rethink this driving idea.

WHY GO IT ALONE

Believe it or not, everyone is not cut out for the solitude of a quiet lunch at a sidewalk café, uninterrupted conversation with one of the locals, or an afternoon reading a good book on the lawn of a mountaintop chalet that is not listed on the Internet or in any brochure printed in the U.S.

When you go it alone, you will miss many of the advantages of traveling with a larger group. You'll miss the camaraderie of touring with many less-than-perfect strangers; miss "The Snorer" in the adjoining aisle on the touring bus; and miss the endless pictures shown by "Grandma-Gertie" of her little Ernie the prodigy. Don't worry about being lonely at mealtime; there will always be 35 other familiar faces crammed in a dining room meant for 12. Expect the coziness of sitting on your bag in a lobby of the hotel with 33 others, waiting for Wilbur and Kate, who forgot to set their alarm. And, oh those daily bag-sorting parties you have every time you move into a new hotel. I promise, no matter how unique your luggage, there will be 87 other bags just like yours.

If solo and you are "Norm-the-Non-smoker," you will miss Sam, who sneaks into the bus bathroom for a malodorous cigarette thinking no one else notices. "Sam-the-Smoker," if you are with the herd, brace yourself for the incessant snide comments from the non-smokers, particularly the indignant ones who quit just last year/month/week/yesterday. Common to every group are "Crying-Carrie," "Hacking-Hal," and of course "Joking-Jed" who has a million, off-color jokes, each lasting longer than this chapter. And…I am willing to bet that if you have been on one of these trips, you have a face for each character I named, plus a few more.

HOW MUCH WILL IT COST?

The first question is always, "How much will it cost?" I hate to sound like a used car salesman, but how much you spend, depends on how much you want to spend. The length of your stay, your standards for accommodations, meals, and how jazzy that car you plan to rent will be are among the considerations that will determine the cost of this or any trip. The following pages will give you some insight as to how you can control those costs and find the best deals.

The cost of renting a car and insurance isn't cheap. But neither is buying Eurail Passes or airline tickets. Your savings will multiply exponentially with the size of your traveling group.

Have you ever dreamed of buying a diamond in Antwerp or a fine watch in Switzerland? While the economy and money exchange rate remain in a constant state of flux, you need to know that if it is expensive in the states, it is probably going to be expensive in Amsterdam or Zurich. You will, however, have the satisfaction of getting that special something at the source country. A little white lie to your friends about the price never hurts (unless they ask you to pick one up for them on your next trip).

TIP: Know the home prices before you go. I planned to buy a Rolex during my first trip to Zurich, but quickly learned I could buy one much cheaper from that guy in a trench coat on the street corner in New York City.

If you do plan to shop for a special, expensive item, check your hometown stores. Know its relative value. Sometimes bringing home a shopping trophy is more important than the cost; that is not necessarily a bad thing. Just make an educated purchase decision. Also, consider the warranty issues. There are plenty of factory authorized Rolex repair centers in the U.S. The warranty issues on a cuckoo clock may be an entirely different matter. Undoubtedly, there will come a time when you just have to make that impulse buy. In most cases, Internet cafés are nearby and offer an excellent opportunity to ensure you are getting a reasonable deal. Lastly, if it needs to be shipped home, know the shipping costs before you break out your wallet. Shipping costs alone have been known to stop husbands' hearts (see Chapter 5, Health Insurance).

JUST IN CASE YOU WERE WONDERING: I still do not own a Rolex.

WHEN TO GO

Generally, tourist seasons are rated as High Season and Low Season. These are the generic terms that dictate travel prices of airline tickets, hotel rooms, car rental costs, and restaurant tabs. High equals expensive. Low is less expensive.[2]

[2] Appendix B in the back of this book is a worksheet to help you wade through the High and Low Tourist Season costs to determine the best time to vacation based on where you want to go and your available dates.

Depending on the exact dates and where you are going, the savings may be extreme or moderate. Typically, in Europe you will find the summer months are the High Season. It is the law of supply and demand. School is out and more people take their vacations in the summer. The weather in Europe is cooler and many are escaping the June to September heat waves. Because of the magical scenery and world-class snow skiing prospects, the Christmas season is also considered a High Season in many areas. Check the major hotel directories in the countries or cities you wish to visit. The tourist seasons are given by exact dates. One week earlier or later could easily double your cost. The fact that there are fewer tourists during the Low Season is an additional bonus. The locals will be more patient with you as they are less stressed and eager to earn your dime. The best rooms are often waiting for you at reduced prices, and you will have the pick of the rental cars.

A word of caution – consider the chances of becoming snowed in and the dangers of driving on icy roads during the midwinter months. Effects of snow and ice far exceed the driving talents of many American tourists.

WHERE DO WE STAY

I'm not sure who did the planning for hotels across Europe, but they did a great job. Hotels of every description, single rooms, and youth hostels are abundant throughout the continent. Reservations through travel agencies or on the Internet are easily made, but you may be paying more for their advertising than the quality of your room. Remember my first sentence, "It's the journey, not the destination…" Finding that perfect Bed and Breakfast may become your fondest memories. Hang around and, in the pages that follow, I will bring you up to speed on what to look for and beware of.

TO DRIVE OR NOT TO DRIVE

Ask yourself, "Is it my intent to see the Sistine Chapel, the Rosetta Stone and the Glockenspiel?" If that is all you want from your vacation, the rails may be for you. However, if your plans include learning the culture, meeting people that are not jaded by hordes of thoughtless American tourists, eating what the locals eat and living the history, then read on.

"There is nothing to fear, but fear itself." Particularly considering the times, I doubt that F.D.R. would have ever thought these words would be used in a book about vacationing in Europe. But, they are just as poignant here as they were in 1941. And that is what this book is about. Driving through Europe is no easier or harder than taking a vacation right here in Hometown USA. Some of the rules, signs and customs are different, but stay with me. Common sense is your biggest ally. You have just begun preparation for an exciting and fun vacation. And, you will be in the driver's seat.

2 DRIVING LAWS
WHAT'S SO DIFFERENT ABOUT DRIVING IN EUROPE?

More people will die from hit-or-miss eating than from hit-and-run driving. (Duncan Hines)

COMMON COURTESY- IT'S THE LAW

Europe is a land of narrow roads, blind curves and roundabouts. You will see more about the roundabouts later. Aside from the traffic laws of the region, common courtesy is the key factor that makes it possible for the efficient traffic flow in Europe. When a slower car moves out of our way, we view it as an unexpected consideration. In Europe, that is the norm, it is expected, it is the law.

PASSING LANE

When you are driving on the Autobahn, Dual Carriage Way, Autostrade, or expressway by any other name, only use the Passing Lane for passing. Because you are driving the speed limit does not give you the right to dominate the passing lane. The next time you are on your U.S. interstate, watch the driving habits of those around you. You will see a number of cars that never leave the passing lane, regardless of how many vehicles are backed up behind them. In Europe, this is not politeness, *it is the law*, and it is enforced.

ROAD SIGNS

Appendix D is a comprehensive listing of road signs you will find while driving in Europe.

PRIORITY LANES - RIGHT OF WAY

In rural areas, as well as congested towns and cities, roads are often so narrow that two cars cannot pass without one pulling over. Priority signs establish the right-of-way. A red circle with a red arrow pointing the direction you are driving indicates that you must yield to on-coming traffic. A blue sign with a white arrow pointing the direction you are traveling indicates you have the right-of-way, or as they say in Europe, *Priority*. If you encounter a situation and you are not sure who has priority, remember, you are on vacation; there is no rush. Pull over and yield to the on-coming traffic. Check Appendix C, Traffic Signs, for a complete listing of Priority Signs.

HORNS AND FLASHING LIGHTS

In most European countries, blowing your horn is only allowed for extreme emergencies. It is *verboten* (German for forbidden). Flashing one's headlights is the accepted method of signaling or trying to get the attention of another. Rest assured, if you linger a little too long in the passing lane on Germany's Autobahn, you will see flashing headlights in action.

TRAFFIC LIGHTS

Remember Toto; you're not in Kansas anymore. I suspect most people are used to finding traffic lights out in the middle of intersections, hanging from horizontal poles or wires, and easy to see. In many European intersections you will have to actively seek out the traffic lights. They may be on a post at the corner nearest you, on a post across the intersection, or even attached to an adjacent building. In many towns you may find a miniature traffic light at your eye level that will be separate from the primary traffic light. It is both an aid to the pedestrian traffic and helps when there is a harsh glare or the primary traffic light is hard to see for other reasons.

Green still means *Go*. Amber (contrary to the beliefs of many) means *Stop if you can, the light will soon be Red*. Red means *Stop*. In some European countries, the Red light will be followed by a Red+Amber sequence. This prepares drivers to get ready to go - Kinda' like, "On your mark, get set, go!" And go they do. Europe is not the place to take red light running lightly. If you are lucky enough not to have an accident, you may be photographed as you pass through the red-lighted intersection. (See Traffic Enforcement Cameras below.)

Right on Red? Throughout Europe, turning right on a red light is prohibited unless there is an additional Green Arrow.

TRAFFIC ENFORCEMENT CAMERAS

England leads the world in the development and use of Close Circuit Television (CCTV). One of the CCTV uses the UK pioneered and uses is the traffic enforcement camera. This technology is also rapidly gaining ground throughout continental Europe and the U.S. CCTV cameras are posted at intersections photographing tag numbers and drivers running red lights - instant fine. Speeders on many highways are similarly photographed along with a recording of their speed - Busted!

If you think you have a free ride because you are in a rental car, think again. The rental car agency you are dealing with is responsible for the payment of the fine, and they have your credit card number. Rest assured, somewhere in your car rental contract is a sneaky little statement holding you responsible for any traffic fines or other charges levied against their car.

ROUNDABOUTS

European roundabouts have long been the topic of legends and horror stories, told by drivers who happened upon them without warning, training, or experience. One's first experience in a roundabout will be confusing at best. However, the simple truth is that roundabouts have proven to be an excellent traffic control device that allows intersections to flow very efficiently and safely. Expect to see roundabouts more and more in the U.S. in years to come. Consider this to be your introduction, *Roundabout 101*.

Roundabouts efficiently move traffic through an intersection without the need for traffic signals. Except in the very congested areas, vehicles can maneuver busy intersections by merely slowing down, instead of stopping for a stop sign or traffic light. Surveys in Europe and the U.S. consistently show that roundabouts increase road capacity and reduce vehicle accidents.

WHICH WAY TO GO

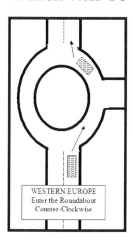

WESTERN EUROPE
Enter the Roundabout
Counter-Clockwise

In the countries that drive on the right side of the road, the vehicles within the roundabouts travel in a counter-clockwise direction or turn right when you enter the roundabout.

In the United Kingdom, Ireland, or anywhere else they drive on the ~~wrong~~ (oops) left side of the road, the vehicles circle in a clockwise direction, or turn left when you enter the roundabout.

UNITED KINGDOM
Enter the Roundabout
Clockwise

If you are directionally challenged and looking for some sort of logic out of all this, you are in luck. Simply stated, you turn in the direction that does not cross the path of any other traffic. It is this simplicity that makes it all work.

RIGHT-OF-WAY

In most countries, the vehicles in a roundabout have the right-of-way over the entering vehicles. Exceptions:

Greece - the vehicles entering the roundabout have the right-of-way over the vehicles already circling.

Netherlands and Italy - right-of-way is determined by posted traffic signs; however, when no signs are posted in Italy, the vehicles entering have the right-of-way, and in the Netherlands, the vehicles already in the circle have the right-of-way.

CLOCK SYSTEM

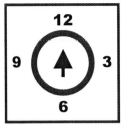

For those who drive the same roundabouts every day, negotiating them is a piece of cake. But approaching a roundabout in an unfamiliar land can be a little daunting to say the least. The co-pilot must be able to quickly and accurately relay information to the driver about which way to turn. My wife still does not understand why pointing or nodding in a direction will not suffice as I am trying to shift gears, avoid sheep in the road and get a good look at the blond in my rearview mirror. And...don't get me going about which way is east or west. We found the old military clock method works very well when approaching roundabouts.

Rule 1: Consider yourself always heading 12 o'clock. If your co-pilot wants you to turn left, then the direction 9 o'clock is given. A right turn command is 3 o'clock and 6 o'clock probably means you missed your turn

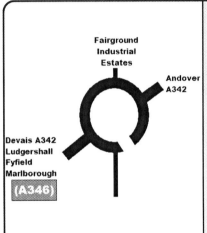

Now, take a look at the sign to the left. It is typical of a sign you may encounter before a roundabout. When orienting yourself to the sign, you are always approaching from the sign's 6 o'clock. A turn to Andover is 2 o'clock, Marlborough, 7 o'clock.

Another interesting note about this sign is the break in the circle. This does not mean traffic stops there; it is a reminder to us Yanks that we need to go LEFT! This directional aid does not appear on every sign, so know which way you need to turn before you get to the roundabout.

If you plan to have your partner act as your navigator, it may be a good idea to take a couple practice drives experimenting with the clock method before you leave for Europe. With a little practice, you will find your communication skills greatly improved. Of course, this only applies to communication skills relative to driving; please consult your Yellow Pages under "Psychologists" if you want to get into the more touchy-feely communication disciplines.

DRINKING AND DRIVING

At first blush, one will find attitudes in Europe toward alcohol much more liberal that in the U.S. It is common for people of a much younger age to have a glass of wine with a meal, and, bars, pubs and beer gardens abound. Touring vineyards, tasting wine and experiencing the endless variety of beers across the continent are a big part of many travelers' experiences. However, if you plan to drive, understand that the laws concerning intoxication are more stringent in Europe than we usually find in the U.S., and the criminal consequences can be quite severe. Do not count on the U.S. Embassy to bail you out. They will ensure you are treated fairly and humanely, but will not interfere with a host country's normal criminal process.

In most of the states in the U.S., it is illegal to drive if your blood alcohol level (BAC) is .08% or higher. While levels will vary from person to person, typically a 160 pound male will have a BAC of .08% after consuming three ounces of alcohol, the equivalent of three 12 ounce beers within an hour. Again, these are averages. Your personal tolerance to alcohol may be more or less.

By contrast, most European countries consider the level of intoxication at .05%, or two drinks by our hypothetical 160 pound male. Of all the wonderful places to visit throughout Europe, neither hospitals nor jails are on the list. If you are going to pop a cork, plan on using public transportation or drink within walking distance of your hotel. It is just not worth the risk.

3 PLANNING THAT TRIP

WHAT TO BUY EARLY ON

It takes as much energy to wish as it does to plan.
(Eleanor Roosevelt)

BUY THIS BOOK

If you are, at this moment, in your favorite bookstore browsing the travel section and seriously considering a driving vacation in Europe, BUY THIS BOOK. You will want to read it a couple times, refer to it while planning your trip and take it with you for a quick reference as you encounter those confusing European road signs that will make perfect sense by the end of your trip.

PASSPORT

Get it *early*; you can't leave home without it. All the information you need to obtain a passport may be found at **http://travel.state.gov/passport/index.html**. Typically, it takes about six weeks to get a passport, but for an extra charge, one may be obtained in about two weeks. But...I'd really hate to gamble my dream vacation on a well-intentioned governmental promise. Best advice - get it NOW.

> **TIP:** When you travel, make several copies of your passport, and put a copy in each of your bags. If you lose the original, take a copy to the nearest U.S. Embassy immediately. The passport copy will help them process your replacement.

DRIVER LICENSE - INTERNATIONAL DRIVER PERMIT (IDP)

First of all, ensure your state driver license will be valid through the return date of your vacation. Most European countries will accept your U.S. driver license; however, there are countries that do require an International Driving Permit (IDP). IDPs are honored in more than 150 countries outside the U.S., including every country listed in this book. These licenses supplement your state driver license, they are not intended to replace valid U.S. state driver license. You must present your state license with the International Driving Permit.

"So why bother?" you ask. Good question! IDPs function as an official translation of your U.S. driver license into 10 foreign languages. Seven countries listed in this book require an IDP; and, there are a few car rental companies that demand both IDP and a valid state driver license before releasing the car to a foreign renter. Purchasing your IDP prior to departure can ward off many potential hassles.

Before you leave on your vacation, you may obtain an IDP from one of the two agencies authorized by the U.S. Department of State. The only authorized distributors of IDP's in the U.S. are the American Automobile Association (AAA) and the American Automobile Touring Alliance (AATA).

- AAA (American Automobile Association), 1000 AAA Drive, Heathrow, FL 32745-5063. Online applications are available on the Internet at **http://www.aaa.com**.
- American Automobile Touring Alliance (AATA), 1151 E. Hillsdale Blvd., Foster City, CA 94404, telephone: 800-622-7070; fax: 650-294-7105

To apply for an international driving permit, you must be at least 18 years old, present two passport-size photographs and your valid U.S. license. It will cost you less than $20.

MORE THAN YOU WANTED TO KNOW: Article 24 of the United Nations Convention on Road Traffic (1949) authorizes the U.S. Department of State to empower certain organizations to issue IDPs to those who hold valid U.S. driver licenses.

International Driving Permit (IDP) Highlights[1]:

- Accepted in over 150 countries outside the US
- Legal I.D.
- Translates into ten foreign languages
- Valid for up to one year
- Must be accompanied by a valid U.S. driver license at all times
- AAA and AATA are the only authorized issuing agencies

CAUTION: There are a lot of private companies out there that will be glad to take your money for an official looking document they claim to be an International Driver Permit. These imitations, or should I say counterfeits, will not be accepted in countries requiring an I.D.P. **Only obtain your IDP from one of the two companies listed above.**

TRAVEL INSURANCE

The cost of your airline tickets, hotel reservations, and car deposit represent a significant investment. If you are a prudent shopper, you will find many great

[1] Source: U.S. State Department: *http://travel3.his.com/travel/tips/safety/safety_1179.html*

deals, but the best deals often have a large stamp across the contract: NO REFUNDS. Buy your airline tickets, make your hotel reservations, and rent your car **before** purchasing your travel insurance policy. Now - if you experience a qualifying reason to cancel your trip such as a serious injury, illness or death in the family, most of your expenses should be recoverable.

Because I believe insurance is such an important topic and takes up so much space, it will be addressed in the next chapter as a topic of its own.

POCKET TRANSLATOR

There are several Pocket Translators on the market in five or more languages. The prices range from $20 to $200 and up. We've made three successful trips on a $20 model. After realizing what we thought was going to be a filet mignon and turned out to be duck liver, my wife demanded an upgrade. She ate the duck liver, I bought the new translator.

There is another advantage we learned about using pocket translators you may never see written anywhere else. As American tourists, our reputation often precedes us and that is not always a good thing. In virtually every case, when we pull out our translator and try to communicate with the locals on their terms, the response has been friendly and as helpful as possible. Ordering dinner, looking for a bathroom, and trying to buy fresh cherries at a local stand have evolved into some of our best travel stories.

MAPS

The value of a good map should never be underestimated. Once you have decided where you are going to go, the selection of a good map will be one of your salient decisions. Brace yourself for sticker shock, maps ain't cheap. Expect to pay between $11.00 and $15.00 per map. I've found *Michelin, BeNeLux, Hallwag* and *ADAC* print the most informational maps. You can find these maps in your local bookstores in the U.S. or you can wait until you get to Europe; they are about the same price. However, if you wait until you are at your destination you will lose the opportunity to use your maps while planning your trip.

NOTE: You may also find maps printed by U.S. companies that are completely in English. Many of the European cities, and even countries, spell their names very differently than we do in the U.S. For example, Germany is *Deutschland* to the locals, and Munich is *München*. These become important issues as you are cruising down the Autobahn at warp speed whilst looking for that town on your American map called Antwerp; and, you do not see anything close to that spelling on any road sign.

Take it from one that has tried, do not bother looking for a cheaper map or, even worse, going without. Driving in Europe is different than anywhere in the U.S. Streets and highways change names and numbers for no apparent reason. I once followed what appeared to be the same street in Munich that changed its name every block.

Limited access highways, what we call an "Interstate" in the U.S., may be referred to as an *Autobahn, Autostrade, Motorways, Autoroutes, Anschluss,* or *Carriageway,* depending on where you are driving. Where they differ, however, is an Autobahn will often abruptly end at the edge of a city and pick up on the other side. With a good co-pilot, one can usually find the way through the town and back on the Motorway by following the directional signs. (Kinda like following breadcrumbs left by the road builders.)

Should you decide to venture into a larger town or city to catch a museum or special sight, tourist maps are generally available at bargain rates and will probably get you through the day. Nearly every city in Europe has a Town Center (look for the signs saying "CENTRE" or a graphic circle that looks similar to a bull's-eye). Most often, the Town Centre is where you will find Information Centers, Tourist Centers, train stations (or directions to), public parking for a price, hotels, shops and, of course, some great sidewalk cafés. Most have some sort of touristy city map available.

GPS

I could not write this section without commenting on the emerging GPS technology for the driving enthusiast. GPS is short for Global Positioning System and translates into a little device you can suction-cup to your windshield that will guide you through the highways and byways of nearly every part of the world including most back city streets. All you have to do is select an address, street intersection, business name, or query by category (gas, food, lodging, etc) and selections appear, nearest to furthest.

In the past couple years, the availability, simplicity and cost of using GPS for private travel have improved dramatically. The leading manufacturers include

Garmin, Lowrance, Magellan, Navman and TomTom.

The cost of portable GPS units range from $200 - $1,000. For $200 you get a portable GPS that has most of the U.S. highways and major roads. You must load the local streets from a computer by region with the provided map supplements. Starting around $600 a unit will include nearly every street in the U.S. (my choice).

Most portable GPS units currently being sold have the capability of inserting an additional memory card loaded with maps of areas not covered in the normal programming. Depending on the brand of GPS you purchased, an add-on map of Europe may cost you $150 - $500.

Many cars come with a built in GPS system and most car rental companies offer this option for an additional charge. They are simple to use and may be easily programmed to speak and view in English. This very well may be your least expensive option.

> **MORE THAN YOU WANTED TO KNOW:** Originally designated the **NAVSTAR** (Navigation System with Timing And Ranging) Global Positioning System, GPS was developed by the US Department of Defense to provide all-weather round-the-clock navigation capabilities for military ground, sea, and air forces. As of this writing, GPS employs 24 spacecraft in 20,200 km circular orbits inclined at 55 degrees. These spacecraft are placed in 6 orbit planes with four operational satellites in each plane. All launches have been successful except for one launch failure in 1981. The full 24-satellite constellation was completed on March 9, 1994. (NASA, 2005)

PARK-AND-RIDE

Beware! Some European cities are horrendous to drive in. Imagine New York City traffic jams on steroids. Remember, these towns and their buildings are hundreds of years old. The streets were originally designed for horse drawn carts, pedestrians and bicycles; and, there may be little or no parking. Driving in larger European cities should be done only by professionals, never attempted by fledgling-American-Euro-drivers. (Oxford, do you hear me?) You may see signs on the highways outside the town asking visitors to "Park and Ride." As the FBI says, "This is a clue."   Public transportation in European cities has been refined to an art. Catch a bus or train to the Town Centre, pick up a map and start from there. You will be amazed at how many sites are within walking distance or a quick bus ride. There are two important rules to remember when you do Park-and-Ride:

1. Know what time the last bus/train goes back to where you parked your car.

2. Know where you parked your car!!! Write it down. Get the street, intersecting street, station name, grid coordinates, or whatever else you need to get back to your car.

CLOTHES

You should be able to get by with two or three days worth of clothes. Laundromats are common throughout Europe. Take a book and enjoy the time to sit back and relax. This too can become another enjoyable diversion during your vacation.

Check the average temperatures for the time of year and location you will be traveling and pack for that temperature. Remember, Europe reads its temperatures in Celsius. Conversion tables are in the back of this book, Appendix B. If it turns out to be a little cooler or warmer than expected, you can always pick up a sweater or pair of shorts during your travels. Select clothes that fit comfortably, are machine washable, and will come out of a suitcase looking presentable. Do not take the label's word for it. Pick a garment, wash it, dry it, roll it up and stuff it in a shoe box. If you would not wear it the next day, don't pack it. While blue jeans wear like iron, they are bulky in a suitcase, heavy and not very warm on the ski slopes.

All too often we pack an outfit for each occasion. That just does not work for an active trip. Pick one or two of your favorite basic colors for pants/shorts, shoes and purses and develop variety through your selection of shirts and blouses. If going to a cooler area, find a jacket that works with slacks, skirts, a dress or jeans. Tweeds or leather work well, tweed is lighter. Wool scarfs and light shawls make excellent accessories, and work well for a little night chill or blasting air conditioners. A wrinkle-free LBD (little black dress) with a nice necklace looks great any night, and a floppy hat and sandals will get you through any occasion during the day.

There are many durable, lightweight blended fabrics on the market that make packing much easier. These fabrics are lighter, take less space in your suitcase, dry quickly and wear like iron. Some clothing retailers specifically sell clothes designed for the traveler.

Europe is a little more formal than some of us are used to. Shorts and flip-flops are a definite No-No in most churches and museums. Restaurant guests are expected to at least wear slacks in the evening and a nice polo shirt. A nice blouse and skirt are always acceptable for women during the evening hours.

Following is an example of how to pack that suitcase.

MEN	WOMEN
1 pair dark blue or black slacks	1 basic little black dress (reversible is great)
2 pair dark colored shorts	1 pair dark slacks
3 polo shirts	2 pair dark shorts
1 light weight, water repellant jacket	3 comfortable tops
1 pair dark socks	1 light weight, water repellant jacket
3 pair white socks	3 pair white socks
4 pair of underwear	4 days underwear
1 pair walking/hiking shoes	1 pair tennis/walking shoes
	1 pair flat dress shoes

Appropriate adjustments are obviously in order if your plans include time on a snowy mountain top. When planning a one or two day ski trip during an otherwise warm-climate vacation, bib and coat rentals may be the better option.

And...a quick word about your jewelry. Leave the expensive stuff at home. Unless you are planning on having an audience with the ambassador, a $10 *Timex* or *Casio* will do just fine. A nice set of faux pearls or inexpensive gold plated necklace are all you should need.

CRIME TIP: The best way not to be selected as a victim is not to have anything worth stealing. And, if a piece of inexpensive costume jewelry is stolen, you lose nothing.

PACKING RULES

1. If it doesn't all fit in one small suitcase, unpack and purge until everything fits.
2. If you are not sure you will wear an item, put it back in the closet.
3. Zip-Lock bags. Bring lots of zip-lock bags. They will keep your personal documents protected from moisture. Protect the rest of your wardrobe; use them to pack fluids such as shampoo, mouthwash, and medications.

FIRST AID KIT

For the most part, your first aid needs should be minimal; but it is nice to have the necessities at hand. Six of the countries featured in this book require first-aid kits in all cars. Should you rent a car from one of these countries, the rental company will most likely include the kit; however, if you are frequently crossing borders, you may have to provide one yourself. There are several first-aid kits prepared commercially, but they are expensive and may not meet your specific needs. Then too, there is the first-aid-kit-explosion-factor: Once opened, commercially packed kits will never fit back into their original containers. Consider making your own kit.

Common items include band-aids (of every shape and size), sterile gauze, first-aid tape, a tube of antibiotic ointment, anti-nausea tablets, motion sickness medication, eye drops, Benedryl cream and Benedryl tabs for allergy attacks, calamine lotion for the itchies and, aspirin and/or Tylenol. Should you run into an unexpected need, the pharmacists in Europe are very helpful and all common over-the-counter medications are available, so there is no compelling reason to pack a gallon jug of *Pepto Bismol*.

Pack sufficient prescription medications to get you through your vacation and an extra week, just in case. The official mantra is to carry all prescription meds in their original containers. Should you opt to pack non-narcotic medications in one of those daily-reminder-containers, be sure to have a copy of the label or prescription packed with the meds. If your prescriptions include narcotics or narcotic derivatives, leave them in their original container. The customs people deal with these issues daily, but there is no fudge-factor when narcotic drugs are concerned.

Pack like items (all size band-aids for example) in smaller, clear zip-lock baggies. Then pack everything in a larger, heavy duty, clear plastic bag. I found one of those cosmetic bonus bags my wife came home with works great. The clear plastic bags make it easy to find what you want, protect from cross contamination, and are appreciated by the Customs guys at the airport. The flexibility of the container makes it a snap to stuff in the corner of any suitcase.

If you plan to put the first-aid kit in your carry-on bag, remember: NO scissors, NO scalpels, NO knives, NO sharpies, NO cigarette lighters, NO guns, NO toy guns. Why *start* your vacation with a *stop* at the airport security checkpoint?

VOLTAGE CONVERTERS - PLUG ADAPTER

Converters - Adapters, they are not the same! Converters convert available voltage to another voltage and plug adapters simply allow you to access the available current to use with your equipment.

The U.S. standard outlet supplies 110 volts (read: 110 v.) 60 cycles of electricity. Europe, on the other hand, typically supplies 220/240 v. 50 cycles. The whys and hows are not important. But you do need to plan ahead to use electronic devices you cannot live without. And to make things worse, different countries use different type plugs. Inexpensive adapter kits come with an assortment of plugs and can be found at any travel or electronic store.

Before packing that equipment, check your owner's manual for specifics! It doesn't take more than a nanosecond to fry your laptop or camcorder if you do not take the proper precautions.

For the most part, anything that runs on a battery will not be a problem, so long as the charger can be set for 220/240v. Most likely, you will only need a plug adapter. Many newer devices such as laptop computers and camcorders are designed to be sold and used worldwide. They will sense and adjust to the voltage automatically. If possible, when charging your battery, you may want to remove it from the device to ensure a power surge does not fry a camera or computer. Actually, this is pretty good information, even in the U.S. Best advice: Carefully read your *Owner's Manual* if you have any doubts or concerns.

Excellent worldwide converter-adapter kits are on the market for less than $50. Typically, the converter has a maximum range of 1600 watts and includes adapter plugs for most applications. They can be found at most travel, electronic stores and some of the larger discount stores.

 CAUTION: The hair dryer is the most problematic of all devices. They pull a lot of power and often exceed the limitations of many of the smaller converters. American hairdryers have been rumored to destroy the entire electrical system of many European roadhouses. You may be able to find a hairdryer that will convert between 110v. and 240v. with the flip of a switch at your local super-center. Most hotels in Europe provide hairdryers; not as a gesture of good will, but to protect their electrical systems from vain American tourists. If you cannot find a convertible hairdryer in the U.S. and must have your own, buy a cheap one when you get to Europe.

FOREIGN CURRENCY

Fortunately, most countries in Europe are now using the Euro (€), eliminating the need of exchanging money every time you cross a border. The biggest exception is the United Kingdom who still uses the British pound (£). Wherever you go, it is a good idea to have at least a few hundred dollars worth of the local currency. While your major credit cards and ATM cards are accepted worldwide, you may find some of the best buys and romantic hotels require cash.

Check for service fees before you purchase foreign currency at a bank or foreign exchange counter. You may be donating 5 - 10% of the amount of your exchange to their Christmas party fund. Here are some real figures from a currency exchange counter in the Orlando International Airport on one day in March 2005: "Will buy Euros at 1.190." "Will sell Euros at 1.452." Do the math. That will cost you about 10% to buy currency and 10% to sell when you return. This is not a good travel investment.

Ask your hometown bank about its foreign currency rates. The bank's standard service package may offer foreign currency withdrawal from your checking or savings account with no, or very small, service fees. Above all, get all the facts before placing your order. Carefully read the fine print on your ATM and credit card contracts to determine what, if any, service charges apply to overseas transactions. If you do not like what you see, check their competitors. (I love a free market society.)

Three ways to avoid most of the service fees are: 1) Use your ATM card to obtain foreign currency at your home bank and at ATMs in your destination country. 2) Overseas, when possible, pay for purchases and services with your credit card.

There are a couple of booby-traps to be avoided. Use your ATM card (not your credit card) for cash. In most cases, when using a credit card to obtain cash, you may avoid the exchange service fee but accumulate an exorbitant cash-advance fee. Also, understand that each overseas ATM transaction may cost as much as $5, so make the best use of them. 3) If your bank charges a small, or no service fee to withdraw foreign currency from your checking or savings account, you should be able to deposit it back into your checking account at the same rate when you return. Again, check with your bank for its particular policies and shop around if necessary.

CHECKLIST:

Take this page to your local copy machine and print a duplicate; you will want to use it again in years to come. The first seven items are in a specific order. You will be well advised to remain in this order.

_____ This Book (thank you)

_____ Passport - if you have one, check the expiration date

_____ International Driver Permit - remember they are only valid for one year

_____ Airline Tickets

_____ Car Rental

_____ Hotel Reservations (if you absolutely must)

_____ Travel Insurance (after air tickets, car rental and hotel reservations are confirmed)

_____ Pocket Translator

_____ Maps

_____ Travel Clothes (stay with basic styles and they will be ready to go next time)

_____ First Aid Kit

_____ Electrical Converter-Plug Adapter Kit

_____ Currency Exchange

4 PLANNING THAT TRIP II
AIRFARE, CAR RENTALS AND HOTELS

*I have a lovely room and bath in the hotel. It's a little
inconvenient, they're in two separate buildings!*
(Henny Youngman)

In a nutshell, the cost of your airline tickets and rental car will be driven (pun intended) by two factors: the season; and, your destination. Further, airlines must consider the day of the week and passenger class you wish to fly. The type of car you hope to drive also influences rental car prices.

AIRFARE

Without a doubt, if you do not watch for the best available fares, the tourist seasons, and day of the week you fly, your airline ticket could be the biggest expense of your vacation. It is not necessary to spend fortunes just to get there. Get on the Internet, or telephone and use your worksheet (Appendix B) to determine the best time of the year and the best day to fly. There are many websites dedicated to discount airline tickets such as Expedia.com, Priceline.com, Travelocity.com, and Orbitz.com, to name a few. Occasionally, the airline ticket counters can find even better deals, but be prepared to pay a counter fee if you purchase your tickets through them. The prices change almost daily, so do not be in a rush. By waiting a few days, you stand a good chance getting a better price.

SOME ADVICE ABOUT AIRLINE TICKETS: Be sure you can get the time off from work before you book those tickets. Most discount airline tickets are non-refundable and there are substantial charges for changing the dates. If you are booking tickets months ahead of time, be sure the airline you are dealing with is not about to go into receivership. For the most part, reading the headlines in the financial pages will keep you out of trouble, but occasionally surprises do spring up. The next chapter deals with Travel Insurance, which may reimburse your losses due to airline financial failure, serious injury or illness, etc. Read that section closely.

AIRPORT TIP: You can make the process of clearing airport security as easy or as hard as your heart desires. The Transportation Security Agency (TSA) was created to ensure our flights are as safe as possible. Their secondary mission is to make our airport experience is as stressful as they can make it. It is our obligation to help the TSA on their first priority, and defeat them on the second; so here is what you can do to facilitate both. First of all, know the list of no-nos, items that you cannot take with you on the airplane - not on your person, not in your carry-on bag. Do not try to carry the following items on your person or carry-on baggage: guns, knives (of any size), toy guns/knives, brass knuckles, scissors of any size, explosives or firecrackers, flammable material such as lighter fluid or gasoline, toenail clippers, cork screws, and the list goes on. Effective April 2005, cigarette lighters will not be allowed through the security checkpoints either. If you do bring such an item, you will be given a choice: either drop it in their trash receptacle, put it in your checked baggage if allowed, or take a bus. Guns and explosives will win you a meeting with an FBI agent and provide a whole bunch of new stories for the grandkids. For a comprehensive look at the rules of flying, check out the TSA website at **www.tsa.gov**.

Personally, when I fly, I void my body of any unnecessary metal. All jewelry stays at home. I wear a $10 plastic watch (which keeps better time than my two pound metal diver's watch) and a nylon belt with a plastic belt buckle. Slip-on shoes are a must; no laces, straps or buckles. And, I have a zippered pouch for any change or other items that may not clear the metal detectors, which goes into my backpack long before I get in the security line. My backpack is for food, drink and reading materials only. You will not see me dragging suitcases down the endless corridors of an international airport. All my luggage is checked at the airline baggage counter. I keep hoping that someday they will lose my bags and buy me a whole new wardrobe.

YOUR CAR

As the old adage reads, *If it sounds too good to be true, it probably is.* The Internet is a powerful tool for today's traveler. Much to the chagrin of legitimate travel agents, the Internet has allowed us common folks the ability to shop worldwide for the best travel bargains. Travel agents have one big advantage; they have a better grasp on who provides quality service, and who does not. They know who the frauds are. You and I must dig a little deeper to assure we are not left standing at the curb, literally and figuratively.

The *Yellow Pages* in your local telephone book have several auto rental agencies that operate internationally. By no means would I disparage the honor of the many rental car companies that only have a presence at your destination in Europe. I am confident most are honest companies trying to provide a quality service for a fair price. Distance and language are both barriers to good communication. Should a billing dispute arise at the end of your vacation, you may find it easier to cope with the situation when dealing with a company who has an office in your hometown.

Driving in Europe is often very different than anything you may have experienced in the United States. Many of the roads are very narrow, and parking is often at a premium. Renting that big luxury car is not only expensive, but will be very hard to maneuver. We once saw a sign where gas was 1.26 € (Euros). At first glance, posted gas prices do not seem so bad, translating to $1.55 per gallon, we thought. That is *per liter*! Gas in Europe is extremely expensive by our standards. Three to four times the price in the U.S. is not uncommon at the European pump, giving yet another reason to avoid that Hum-V the kids want you to rent.

If there are just two of you, consider a moderately priced sports car. Nothing matches the exhilaration of driving your honey in a two-seater convertible down Alpine logging roads on a sunny day. A touch of reality: Small cars have tiny storage areas. Darting in and out of those narrow streets and small parking spaces will be a snap, and the gas prices will certainly be a lot easier on the wallet; but, do not make the mistake of dragging your three jumbo suit cases out to the car rental parking lot with the intent of squeezing them into the trunk of an Audi TT. If a sports car is your pleasure, pack light and pack in collapsible or even plastic bags. Much to my delight, I found the smaller car had an added benefit of restricting the items my wife wanted to buy at each and every tourist shop we ventured into. Things were great until the first intuitive shopkeeper offered to ship that Cuckoo clock home for us. That is when my shopaholic wife said, "Check, point, match!"

During your travels, you will surely check into a couple of Bed and Breakfasts (B&B's) where your room is atop a narrow, windy third level staircase. The benefits of luggage restrictions caused by your little car take on an entirely new light by the time you top the second story leading to the third stairway.

Fuddy-duddy, medium sized cars are abundant for that extra passenger and extra suitcases. In actuality, they are the staple of the car rental business in Western Europe. Regardless of the type of car you rent, try your best to ensure your vehicle is equipped with seat warmers. I used to think these butt-warmers were the height of indulgence, until I used one on a cool night in Wales. With the seat turned on high, we cruised with our top down and enjoyed the brisk air while we stayed warm and toasty.

Because of the expensive gas prices, most rental vehicles in Europe have a standard transmission. For those with little or no experience driving a stick shift, this is not a good time to learn. There are simply too many distractions to be bothered with relearning how to drive. Consider leasing an automatic transmission.

IN THE U.K.

Cars in the United Kingdom offer a completely different set of issues. Yes, the steering wheel is on the right side of the car, and yes, the pedals are in the same order as the U.S., gas on the right, brake to the left of the gas, and clutch (if equipped) on the far left. If you get a standard transmission, the gearshift will be between the driver and passenger (the left side of the driver). That becomes extremely confusing and sometimes dangerous for the fledgling American driver. In the U.K., demand an automatic transmission.

RENT OR BUY THAT CAR

Instead of driving an off-the-shelf rental, wouldn't you rather drive your own foreign luxury car across Europe? Many of the finer European automakers have devised an interesting twist combining the sale of a new car with a driving vacation. Mercedes-Benz, BMW and SAAB call their program the *European Delivery Program*, Volvo refers to theirs as *Overseas Delivery* and Porsche touts the *Euro Delivery Program*. Details differ between companies and may change from year to year. The plan is simple: entice a buyer by providing him the opportunity to drive his dream car on the streets it was designed for: the Autobahn, winding Alpine roads or tracing the images of the Grand Prix in Monaco. Packages range from a basic travel allowances to all-inclusive tours. Buyers may be treated to VIP tours of the auto factory, offered meals and provided a travel itinerary envious of any vacationer, including exclusive hotels, top-drawer amenities and the finest local cuisine. Buyers may also enjoy discounts on the sale of an awesome car and shared or free shipping costs. The Internet is an awesome tool for comparing the various programs, however the final deal must be cut at your local authorized dealership. Because the point of purchase is Hometown, USA, the vehicle you purchase must meet all applicable standards, just as if you were to take delivery at home.

TRUST THAT USED CAR DEALER

Planning to buy a used car after arriving on the continent may sound like a good idea, but think long and hard before jumping in with both feet. It sounds like a no-brainer, but *caveat emptor*. Unless you have some excellent contacts in your destination country, you may wish to do some research during your first trip and try this the second time around. If you try to make advance arrangements by telephone, you will most probably find that people are simply not prepared to deal with your issues.

CAUTION: Before you start dialing, consider setting yourself up with some sort of Internet telephone service (see chapter 7).

Although I do not recommend buying a car for first time travelers, I will give you some inside information that may tweak your interest for future trips.

- Most of the automakers we are familiar with in the U.S. also have used car lots in Europe.
- *Autotrader,* the magazine that lists thousands of used vehicles, also distributes their publication throughout Western Europe.
- AIG, America's largest property/casualty insurance company, has a big presence in Europe. Contact information for AIG's European offices may be found on their website at **www.aig.com**.
- Liability insurance (called "Third Party Insurance" in Europe) is the absolute minimum insurance you must carry - and it is absolutely necessary. Is this absolutely clear?
- The European Union has not come to a full agreement about the laws concerning vehicle registration and insurance. The rules are changing almost daily, so if you must buy that used car, be sure to contact your destination country vehicle registration department before committing yourself to a big expense.
- A recent check with Ireland's authorities revealed the tax (license plate) for a 3 liter car is a little over 1,000 €.

Auto Insurance

Standing at the counter of a foreign rental car agency after a ten-hour overnight flight is probably a poor time to make quick financial decisions about your insurance needs. Approach that rental counter knowing what your options are; and, know what insurance options you plan to purchase from the car rental agency.

As I have said earlier, I consider insurance a sacred topic while traveling and address this in detail in the insurance chapter.

Hotels

Of all the things you spend your vacation money on, hotels have the widest cost range. As much as any service, hotels, B&B's and room prices are influenced by the tourist season. Nowhere on earth are there a greater variety of accommodations than Western Europe. Traditional hotels are similar to those in the U.S.: plush to seedy and everything in between. Often, the price will include your night's lodging and a heavy continental breakfast.

Bed and Breakfasts are seldom hard to find, clean and moderately priced. Their name is exactly as it implies: a place to stay and breakfast in the morning. They are similar to those in the U.S. in that the buildings are generally very old and decorated/furnished with antiques common to the area. You will find the B&B

much more personal. Some even include afternoon tea and optional family-style dinner seating.

Continental breakfasts in Europe often consist of coffee, tea, several types of juices, boiled eggs, an assortment of cereals, yogurt, and a variety of cold cuts, cheeses and breads. Selections may be skimpier in some hotels, and others will offer eggs, pancakes and waffles off the grill. If your continental breakfast is a deal breaker, get all the details before you unload your car.

IMPORTANT (Husbands: A Pitfall to be Avoided)

Rooms, often called "zimmers," are available for those who wish to cut their costs even more. If the proximity of your toilet and shower are of primary consideration, beware. Your privy may be a short walk (or long, depending on your outlook) down the hall and shared by others. Be sure to ask before signing on the dotted line.

Terms To Remember: *"In Suite"* or *"In Suite Accommodations"* mean the privy is in your room. When in doubt, ask before you commit.

Hostels are generally for youthful travelers such as teenagers just out of high school. Several people may share a room and the accommodations are often a little Spartan; but, they are available for almost anyone and many people consider them part of the adventure.

I am going to invent an additional class: "Themed Accommodations." They include castles, haunted houses, bunkers, barges, or just about anything else you can put a bed in and call it home. Imagine feasting with lords and ladies before spending a night in a castle chamber, awakened by the call of wild peacocks. Not in some tourist trap, but in an honest-to-goodness 1,000 year old castle. Many people thrive on castle tours in Scotland, Bavaria, Spain, Poland and other areas of Europe. Others opt to live with ghosts of kings and knights, and prefer to take the haunted house tour, traveling from town to town in search of the ghosts of ancestors past. Others seek a night's lodging upon a barge along one of the many waterways found throughout Europe. Depending on the number of rooms and the amenities, you may find "Themed Accommodations" listed as hotels, castles or bed and breakfasts.

Accommodations are relatively easy to find on the Internet. The luxury hotel chains common to the U.S. may be found throughout Europe if that is your cup of tea. Should you wish to stay in lodging that reflects the region, but feel compelled to make reservations in advance, there are several international chains that have purchased smaller hotels and B&B's. They ensure that quality is maintained and make excellent stopovers. A couple of the more common chains that have excellent establishments throughout Europe are Best Western and Romantic Inns. Reservations can easily be made via the Internet or available toll free telephone numbers.

If you absolutely cannot force yourself to leave without reservations, be sure to book them before purchasing your Travel Insurance (next chapter). Travel Insurance assures you are covered if it becomes necessary to cancel your trip due to an unexpected emergency. Otherwise, you may face significant cancellation penalties.

The one hotel reservation that I do strongly recommend you make is a room at, or as close as possible to the Airport for your last night in Europe. The reduced car rental for that one-day will surely off set any additional expenditures of the airport hotel. You are in for a long flight home. Spending the last night at an airport hotel allows you to turn your car in a day prior, and enjoy a slow paced departure.

5 PLANNING THAT TRIP III
INSURANCE

Picking an insurance policy by only considering its price tag
is like buying a skateboard because it's on sale
when you really need a bus.   *(A Curleyism)*

TRAVEL INSURANCE

Read the newspapers. Bad things happen to people right here in Hometown U.S.A. I say this so as not to create an unnecessary paranoia about traveling, only to motivate you to prepare for your trip. Do not let the "bad things syndrome" kill your dream, but do prepare.

The problem is, in Europe you will be much farther from home. Any problems you encounter may be amplified proportionally by distance. Let's look at a common but serious problem affecting tourists, a debilitating medical problem: You have a stroke in Vienna. Europe is blessed with many fine hospitals and you will receive first-rate attention. But, your hometown health insurance may completely deny coverage outside the United States, or may have (probably has) limitations for overseas incidents. In addition to the expected expenses, the air-ambulance ride home can be financially devastating. A quality travel insurance policy should cover most, if not all expenses you may incur.

PRE-EXISTING MEDICAL CONDITIONS

Talk with a representative about your specific situation before you make your initial deposits if you have a pre-existing medical condition that you feel may be problematic to an insurance carrier. There may be additional costs, time limitations, or you may be denied coverage all together. While you are sitting in an Emergency Room in Sicily is not the time to sort out this matter.

Below is a list of the coverage options you may want to consider when purchasing your travel insurance policy. See individual policies for specifics:

Accidental Death: may also cover loss of arms, legs or sight suffered during an accident while you are on your vacation.

Auto Collision/Damage/Liability: may be obtained through a travel insurance package policy, or separately with your car rental company (see previous chapter). When you intend to rent a car overseas, be sure that you are adequately insured. Your U.S. auto insurance is not always valid in other countries. You may wish to purchase supplemental insurance, which is usually available from most major rental agents.

Baggage Delay: applies when your Rome bound luggage has an unexpected detour to Hong Kong and you need another change of underwear. Additionally, when the bags do arrive, you may be in the next country. This coverage should close the gap with the least expense and inconvenience possible.

Baggage Loss: is the coverage my wife hoped to use when we were on our way to Paris. Unfortunately, the airlines have gotten much better about losing bags. Nonetheless, bags do get lost from time to time. Be sure to read the fine print and understand the clauses about duplicate coverage through the airline.

Dental: coverage may be included with medical coverage or obtained separately.

Medical: coverage is for a sudden and unexpected illness or injury that requires immediate treatment; or dental care to treat a condition resulting from injury or infection, breakage or loss of a filling.

Medical - Emergency Medical Evacuation: coverage is available to cover costs when a serious illness or injury requires immediate evacuation. It may also cover the return of your remains to your residence in the event of your death.

Trip Cancellation: will reimburse most of your prepaid or obligated travel expenses, not because you simply changed your mind, but for good cause, such as serious illness, jury subpoena, strikes, natural disasters, revoked military leave, etc.

Trip Travel Delay: is available for expenses caused by such things as loss of your passport, delays by your airline, and auto accidents, just to name a few.

You may have additional coverage through your homeowner's policy, personal car insurance policy, as a service of your credit cards or through your credit union. Read the small type in your policies and understand *your* coverage.

REMEMBER: Part of what you are paying for is peace of mind and convenience. Even if you know you are covered, ask yourself, "I have two hours to catch my flight and my fender has a new dent. How confident am I that I can quickly clear the car rental counter?"

I am not recommending any specific company to do business with, simply because no one is paying me to advertise their product. (When they say, "It is not about the money" - it **is** about the money.)   Go to your favorite Internet Search Engine and type in "Travel Insurance." You should find a long list of potential insurance carriers with a variety of services and costs. See what policies best meet your needs. Get recommendations from local travel agents and friends that have used them before. Get the facts. All companies are easy to get along with when they are taking your money. The true test of any insurance company is how well they process a reasonable claim. Check the Better Business Bureau and even your local Insurance Commissioner for customer complaints.

- You must purchase your travel insurance package AFTER you have committed to the major expenses of your trip such as airline tickets, hotels, car rental, etc.
- If you have pre-existing medical conditions, be sure to personally speak with an insurance representative before making any final commitments.

The U.S. Department of State has an excellent website dedicated to travel insurance issues and provides up-to-date listings of insurance companies. You may find this web page at **http://travel.state.gov/travel/abroad_health.html**.

AUTO INSURANCE

Auto insurance has two basic components, liability insurance and collision-comprehensive insurance. Every country in the European Union requires third party liability insurance on every car on the road. That cost will most probably be reflected in the price of your rental agreement, but check to be sure. Do not make the mistake of thinking you are also covered for damage done to your rented vehicle.

ABOUT RATIONALIZATION

A conversation in the movie "The Out-of-Towners" provides some insight about our thought process when deciding the need for extra insurance on our rented vehicles:

Car Rental Agent recommending a luxury car: ".... The car practically drives itself. Would you like collision insurance?"

Steve Martin: "Well, if the car drives itself and we have an accident, it will be the car's fault, right?"

Your personal auto insurance may be applicable to rental cars, or may not. Supplemental coverage may also be included through your credit card agreements, your credit union, and fraternal or professional organizations. Even if you know you are covered in the U.S. - Beware! Insurance provided by your personal and supplemental policies may not be valid overseas. When overseas, it might be necessary to purchase auto insurance coverage we normally would not buy when renting a car in the states.

A car I was renting was sideswiped while parked overnight somewhere north of Swansea, Wales. Although I had purchased the rental car company's insurance package, I expected delays when I got to the airport. Much to my surprise, the agency clerk saw the inclusion of their insurance on my rental agreement and I was on my way in about ten minutes, no questions asked. The peace of mind knowing you are well insured may certainly be worth the extra expense.

If you intend to use your travel insurance policy for your rental car, contact your prospective rental car company. Ensure they can quickly process a claim with the travel insurance provider you are considering. Should you need to make an auto-insurance claim, the process will be much easier if the two agencies have a track record of working together.

6 PLANNING THAT TRIP IV
WHERE TO GO AND WHAT TO SEE

You got to be careful if you don't know where you're going, because you might not get there. (Yogi Berra)

Sit back and close your eyes. Where or what in Europe electrifies your imagination? Whether it is the Bavarian Alps, vineyards of France, Swiss chalets, or Spanish castles, that is your starting point. If you have not figured it out by now, I am not an advocate of planning a driving vacation that includes time in the bigger cities. No doubt there are wonderful things to see in many of the larger European cities; the Coliseum in Rome, Louvre in Paris, Tower of London, and more.

What I do suggest is, if you do want to see the sights in the larger cities and drive the countryside, split your vacation and avoid the stress of unthinkable traffic jams and expensive parking fees. London currently levies fees for driving in the city on weekdays and Paris is considering a similar program. The message is clear; there are too many cars for too little space. Use public transportation while in the larger cities, and pick up your rental car when you are heading out into the country.

TOURIST AGENCY PLANNED

There are several ways to plan a driving vacation in Europe. You can turn it over to a tourist agency and let someone else lay out your itinerary, make reservations ahead of you and head to the airport with a pocket full of vouchers to pay for your car, hotels and side trips. You leave home with the confidence of seeing some really nice sites and the comfort of knowing you have a place to stay each night. You will, however, lose the freedom to stay longer in an area that you would like to explore further, and must stay in some locations that simply do not "float your boat." For a first time traveler with little or no direction, this may not be a bad compromise and an excellent way to plan your traveling adventures.

I remember the first conversations with our first Tourist Agent. They reminded me of a quip from *Alice's Adventures in Wonderland* by Lewis Carroll:

"Would you tell me, please, which way I ought to go from here?" [asked Alice].

"That depends a good deal on where you want to get to," said the Cat.

" don't much care where-" said Alice.

"Then it doesn't matter which way you go," said the Cat.

"--so long as I get SOMEWHERE," Alice added as an explanation.

"Oh, you're sure to do that," said the Cat, "if you only walk long enough."

PIN METHOD

The Pin Method is an excellent way to organize or structure a vacation. Do you remember those maps I mentioned in chapter 3? Take a map of the country you plan to visit and staple it to a foam board. Most likely, because you were interested in a certain country or region, there are at least a couple places you have a heightened interest in. Place a pin in those locations and draw a line to the side and make side notes. Talk to anyone and everyone you know who has visited that area and ask them, "What are the three places or things I absolutely must see when I go to...?" Put a pin and make appropriate side comments on each. Read tourist and history literature and seek out additional sites of interest, place your pins and make side comments.

Eventually, you will begin to see groupings of pins. Those are the locations you will most probably want to visit, you will develop a feel for how long you want to stay at each stop, and a logical route of travel will begin to emerge.

The Pin Method is a great way for more than one person to actively participate in the planning of a driving vacation, and if approached with the right mind-set can almost be as much fun as the trip itself.

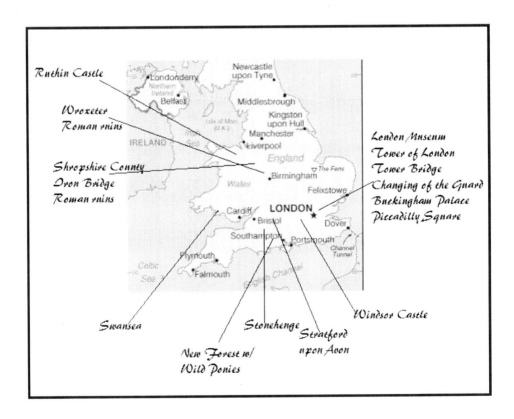

THE "LET'S GO DOWN THAT ROAD" METHOD

For the free spirit, this is the ticket to the perfect vacation. The traveler needs only to arrange for three items: The airline tickets, to have the rental car waiting at the airport, and (optional but recommended) reservations at the airport hotel for the last night in Europe.

The planning couldn't be simpler. Pick a country or region you wish to visit. After looking at a map before driving out of the terminal, find a point on the map that looks interesting and head in that direction. Stop when you see something interesting and find a bed and breakfast when you start to get tired, which is usually pretty early on the first day. From there you have two options, stick around or move on. Talk to the locals, read the literature in the hotel lobby, pick your next destination and go. If you find something interesting on the way, stop and investigate. There are no deadlines and no hotel reservations waiting for you. Your primary concerns include finding the perfect roads to drive and the best lodging facilities for the cheapest prices. No matter where you go - you are there!

This type of vacation planning is, understandably, a little daunting to the beginner. Panic will set in if you have not found accommodations in the first 20 minutes. Fear not, something will be around the next bend. If you do have a hard time finding acceptable accommodations, head toward the nearest large town - something will be there, I guarantee. (Trust me; the check is in the mail.)

7 COMMUNICATING WITH HOME
"E.T. PHONE HOME"

Many attempts to communicate are nullified by saying too much.
(Robert Greenleaf)

For some, the fact that you will be totally out of touch is one of the great benefits of traveling overseas; for others, this thought terrifies them. If you believe in the value of solitude, skip the next few pages; too much information is not a good thing. However, if you find yourself in the latter group, either by choice or necessity, read on.

Technology is moving so quickly, I am hesitant to write this chapter because it very well may be out of date before this book goes to print. Nevertheless, I will discuss some basic ways you can keep in touch with the folks back home; each has its limitations and advantages.

POST CARDS

Post Cards are the old standby. They provide one-way, albeit slow communication. Your friends and family know you are thinking of them and that you are OK. That is making the assumption that you do not arrive home before they receive the card.

EMAIL

Email is the best of both worlds. You can check it when you want, and respond at your leisure. Email machines may be found in nearly every airport and at many tourist hotspots. If you have an Internet account with email at home, you most probably have the ability to access your email account from anywhere in the world. You may connect to your email through the Internet by a process called "web mail." Internet cafés may be found in larger cities and many smaller towns and villages. The cost to use one of their computers is very easy on the pocket. Public computers may also be found in many hotel lobbies, but they are very expensive to use. $5 for 15 minutes is not uncommon in a hotel, compared to $2 for an hour in an Internet café. "Hotspots,"[1] are becoming more and more available in airports, larger cities and many hotels.

Your ability to access your home email account through web mail varies from one Internet company to another, and you will have to check with your own service provider for the specifics. Web mail is a fairly easy process; in a nutshell, here is how it works:

---

[1] Hotspot is a geek word for an area that wireless computer connectability is available. They are common in airports, coffee shops, internet cafés, hotels and many unexpected locations. You must have your own computer, equipped with a wireless networking card to take advantage of a hotspot.

You buy a cup of cappuccino (optional) and rent a computer at the corner café. In the Internet address bar, type in the webmail address given to you by your hometown internet provider. Example - **webmail.your-provider.com**. The next screen will ask for your log-in and password, and you are in. From there you can read, respond and initiate email from your account, just as if you were on your home computer. The key here is, you must get with your internet provider and get instructions about logging on and passwords. Do not be discouraged or intimidated. It is truly a simple process if you will approach it one step at a time.

Internet-Laundromats are the latest rage in Paris and other European towns. Wash your clothes, check your email and review your stock portfolio all in one stop. The only thing missing is a good glass of Chardonnay (which, I guess, you could brown-bag). The point here is that the world is going digital around us, and you will see more and more opportunities to stay connected at places we never expected.

One thing you will find that may put a hitch in your giddy-up, computer keyboards in other countries may be unique to their region. Trying to key on a French keyboard is a unique experience at best. But…that just provided another story over cocktails in the years to come.

LANDLINE OR HARDWIRE TELEPHONE

Just like the U.S., you will find a telephone by the bedside of nearly every hotel. And your hotel will be more than happy to connect you to your international calling destination for a big, BIG cost. If you are planning to communicate internationally using the traditional landline telephone, here are some basic rules:

- Always make your calls from a pay telephone. This disconnects you from the telephone for charging purposes.
- **Never** use your credit card or personal phone card when making international telephone calls. You may unknowingly dial through a service provider that charges exorbitant fees. Once your credit card number or telephone pin number is attached, you are liable for those charges.
- Purchase a long distance telephone card with international calling options, and use it. There are several cards on the market, available at retail stores and warehouse clubs, which offer excellent international rates. And, in the off chance a shady telephone company does latch onto your call, you stand only to lose the amount your card is worth.

Cellular telephone expertise in Europe is top-drawer technology. The Europeans are using hard-line telephones less and less and depending solely upon their cell phones. Many companies are quickly gearing their equipment and services to meet the travelers' needs. Some cell phones in the U.S. are technologically capable of being used in Europe, but most are not; in most cases they are very expensive to use. I suspect this too will be changing in the near future.

In Europe, you will find cell phones available for short-term use that come with prepaid minutes and include overseas calls for a reasonable price. This allows you the convenience we have all become accustomed to with our cell phones and you are instantly available to friends and family back home.

INTERNET TELEPHONY

VoiP is also known as Voice Over Internet Protocol or Broadband Telephone. This is the wave of the future and is quickly becoming more and more popular. There are several types of systems currently available: computer-to-computer, computer to landline and digital telephone. I'll explain each separately.

COMPUTER TO COMPUTER CONNECTION

Computer to computer connection is exactly what the name implies. You must first find a location that you can obtain high speed Internet access, such as an Internet café, airport lobby, hotel, etc. It does not matter if your connection is wired or wireless, but it must be high-speed access. From your computer, you may talk to other people who are on their computer. Both people speak into a computer microphone and hear the other person through the computer speakers or their headset. This technology requires the users to utilize the services of an Internet telephony company. At the time of this writing, a company called Skype (**www.skype.com**) leads the market and offers computer-to-computer Internet telephony service for no charge. Yes, there is no charge for communicating with the guy next door, in Europe, Asia or Australia. The downside is that the person you are calling must be at their computer when you are making the call.

COMPUTER TO LANDLINE

Computer to landline makes it possible to connect to another's home phone or cell phone, in far off places for pennies per minute. This process works very similar to the computer-to-computer format, but you must first pay for talk time, which is very reasonable. Before making your first call, you must open an account and post money to that account. Poof! You are ready to communicate. As before, you must have high-speed Internet access and make the call from your computer using a headset and computer telephony software. You may use your personal laptop or log into the telephony service via the Internet on a public computer. The big difference is the other person does not have to be tied to his or her computer when you are trying to contact them.

DIGITAL TELEPHONE SERVICE - OR - IP TELEPHONE SERVICE

This is another Voice Over Internet Protocol (VoiP) use. It is offered through most broadband Internet service providers and some independent companies. At this time, the most prominent independent company is Vonage (**www.vonage.com**). A telephone adapter is given/sold to customers who use digital telephone service. That adapter, when connected to a standard telephone, converts the telephone's analog signal to the broadband digital connection and visa versa. For pennies a minute, this converter may be used to make telephone calls anywhere in the world. The only requirement is having access to a broadband connection you can hook your telephone adapter to.

CAUTION: There are a few countries around the world that have a government monopoly on telecommunications services and prohibit the use of VoiP telephone connections. While Turkey is the only country featured in this book that has such laws, it would be wise to check before placing your first call in another country.

(Other countries where VoiP is prohibited include Albania, Cuba, Cyprus, Jordan, Kenya, Mexico, Pakistan, Panama, Slovakia, South Africa, Thailand, Venezuela, and Vietnam.)

ON THE HORIZON

There is technology immerging that will marry the use of cellular telephones to VoiP, making it the best of both worlds. No one I've found has ventured to pontificate how this may affect the worldwide traveler, but it can only be in a good way. Give it some time and watch the technical news section of your favorite publications.

MAKING INTERNATIONAL CALLS

Making International telephone calls may seem a little tricky at first. It is much like the combination lock on an elementary school locker - simple to use, but you must know the combination. Appendix C in the rear of this book will cipher the code for you and is an excellent resource for calling to or from Europe. This information applies whether using Ma Bell or VoiP.

SECTION II
THE COUNTRIES

8 AUSTRIA

LOCAL SPELLING: *ÖSTERREICH*
ABBREVIATION: AT

Austria is a land locked at the crossroads of Central Europe with many easily traversable Alpine passes and valleys. The west and south are mostly Alpine mountains contrasting to the eastern and northern part of the country where the terrain is flat or gently sloping. There are an abundance of small villages and towns along the well-maintained highways and roads offering friendly people, great food and landscape too large to capture in any camera. Austria is a country rich in history, architecture and cultural resources. You may even find some of the finest vineyards Europe has to offer. The memory of the Oscar-winning, The Sound of Music movie lingers on, as die hard enthusiasts trek to Salzburg just to take The Sound of Music tour.

When you get near Vienna, be sure to swing by a little town called Grinsing. Grinsing is famous for its Viennese wine taverns or wine restaurants, called a Heurigen, and is a must. Here you can experience the best of Viennese food and traditional music including the Viennese waltz, and test the year's best wines.

If a team of driving enthusiasts ever colluded to invent the perfect motoring experience, their product may very well have been the Grossglockner Road. This is one of Europe's longest and most panoramic alpine highways with curves, bends and hairpin turns; truly the drive of a lifetime. It begins above 2,400 feet at Bruck an der Grossglocknerstrasse, continues through the Hochtortunnel at an elevation of 8,220 feet and ends in the province of Carinthia.

The road conditions in Austria are generally excellent. In the winter months, however, in the mountainous areas they may become dangerous due to snowfall, ice, or avalanches. Some alpine roads may be closed for extended periods of time or require the use of snow tires or chains. Driving in the winter conditions of Austria is not something to be undertaken by drivers inexperienced in this environment.

Summer driving, however, is pure heaven for the driving enthusiast. Get off the major highways and enjoy winding mountain roads and smell the fragrance of the alpine air. Follow the beautiful Danube and discover river castles and stunning views. Live The Sound of Music. Austria will be a drive you will never forget.

FAST FACTS

Area	83,870 Sq. Kilometers/32,382 Sq. Miles A little larger than South Carolina
Primary Language	German
Nationality	*noun:* Austrian(s) *adjective:* Austrian
Currency	Euro (EUR)
Primary Religions	Catholic 74%, Protestant 5%
Population	8,000,000
Capital / Population	Vienna / 1, 5000,000
Other Large Cities / Population	Graz / 220,000 Linz / 190,000 Salzburg / 150,000 Innsbruk / 116,000

DRIVING FACTS

License	Minimum driving age is 18. A U.S. driver license alone is not sufficient to drive in Austria. A valid driver license must be accompanied by an International Driver's Permit (obtainable in the U.S. from the American Automobile Association and the American Automobile Touring Alliance).	
Speed Limits *(If not posted)*	Neighborhoods	As posted
	Built up areas	50 kph / 31 mph
	Major roads outside towns	100 kph / 62 mph
	Highways	130 kph / 80 mph
Speed / Distance	Kilometers Per Hour KPH / Meters – Kilometers	
Side of the Road	Drive on the right side of the road unless One-Way	
Roundabouts	Vehicles in the roundabout have the right-of-way over vehicles entering the circle. When in the roundabout, drive in a COUNTER-CLOCKWISE direction.	
Seat Belts	Front Seats	Required
	Rear Seats	Required if available
	Children	• Under 12 years and less than 1.5 meters are not allowed in front seat unless in an approved seat or harness • Under 12 but over 1.5 meters must use adult belt
Traffic Lights	As in the U.S., <u>Green</u> means GO and <u>Red</u> means STOP. <u>Yellow</u> signals to STOP until the intersection is cleared of traffic. You may then proceed safely. <u>Red+Yellow</u> signal means PREPARE TO GO.	
Right on Red	No	

Required Equipment	Warning triangle
	First aid kit
	Extra bulb kits and fire extinguishers are recommended.
Pedestrians	Pedestrians and bicyclists have an unconditional right-of-way over vehicles turning left or right. Right-of-way in crosswalks is determined by local signage.
Tolls	IMPORTANT: Austria requires all vehicles using the autobahn to display a highway tax sticker "Autobahn Vignette" on the inside windshield of the vehicle. The sticker may be purchased at border crossings, gas stations in Austria, as well as small "Tabak" shops located in Austrian towns. Fines for failing to display a valid autobahn vignette on the windshield of your car are usually around $120.00. If renting your vehicle in a country other than Austria, they most likely will have vehicles that already bear the Austrian tax sticker. Tolls are charged on many of the major highways, including A9, and A10.
Parking	In most of the larger cities, you must pay for street parking. Vouchers may be obtained from any of several parking kiosks and displayed on your dash or visible through the front window. Carefully check for parking instructional signs wherever you park.
Fuel	Unleaded Regular 91 octane — *Bleifrei Normal* Unleaded Super 95 octane — *Bleifrei Super* Diesel — *Diesel*
Motorcycles	Helmets are mandatory Headlights required at all times
Fines	Law enforcement may collect fines during the traffic stop. Be sure to get an official receipt.

Drinking and Driving	You will be considered to be impaired and subject to arrest if your BAC is .05% (.5 mg.ml) or more.
Misc.	Some car rental agencies have strict policies forbidding travel into countries bordering Austria's eastern and southern borders. Simply crossing the border in some locations may be considered auto theft. Even if it is an honest mistake or simple error in judgment, the cost and incontinence may be monumental. Read your contract and abide by the conditions.
U.S. State Department Traffic Safety and Road Conditions	Safety of Public Transportation: Excellent Urban Road Conditions/Maintenance: Excellent Rural Road Conditions/Maintenance: Excellent Availability of Roadside Assistance: Excellent

EMERGENCY TELEPHONE NUMBERS

Police	133
Fire	122
Ambulance	144
Doctor	141
US Embassy	Boltzmanngasse 16 A-1090 Vienna Tel.: (+43-1) 31339-0 Fax: (+43-1) 310 06 82

TERMS OR WORDS YOU MAY SEE ON THE ROAD

English	German
Attention	Achtung
Bed and Breakfast	Gasthaus
Car	Auto
Car Rental Agency	Autovermietung
Caution	Vorsicht
Detour	Umleitung
Diesel	Diesel
East	Osten
Entrance	Eingang / Einfahrt
Exit (roadway)	Ausfahrt
Expressway	Autobahn
Forbidden	Verboten
Gasoline	Benzin
Hospital	Krankenhaus
Hotel	Hotel
Left (direction)	Links
Motor Oil	Motoröl
Museum	Museum
No Parking	Parken verboten
North	Norden
One-way	Einbahnstraße
Parking	Parken
Parking Lot	Parkplatz
Passenger Vehicle	Pkw, Personenwagen
Police	Polizei
Police Station	Polizeistation
Restaurant	Restaurant
Right (direction)	Rechts
Road Closed	Straße gesperrt
Room for Rent	Zimmer zu vermieten
Slow	Geschwindigkeit drosseln / Fahren sie langsamer
South	Süden
Street	Straße (strasse)
Toll Road	Mautstraße
Truck	Lkw, Lastwagen
Welcome	Wilkommen
West	Westen
Yield	Vorfahrt beachten

An excuse you might try if involved in a traffic accident. (According to urban legends, it worked in the U.S.)

Ein Fussänger ist gegen mich geprallt und unter mein auto gepallen.

(Translation: "A pedestrian hit me and went under my car.")

A great opening line for that awkward moment you absolutely cannot think of a way to start a conversation.

Elepanten sind die einzigen tiere, die nicht springen können.

(Translation: "Elephants are the only animal that cannnot jump.")

9 BELGIUM

LOCAL SPELLING: *BELGIQUE/BELGIE*
ABBREVIATION: BE

Belgium - the inspiration of the beautiful yet somber poem *In Flanders Fields*. Flanders is actually western Belgium. The American War Cemetery situated near the village of Waregem, named for the poem, is the final resting place for 368 American soldiers killed during the First World War. Whether you are searching for diamonds in Antwerp, Medieval past, the history of Waterloo and Bastogne, or just a quiet drive on mountain roads, it all is in Belgium.

Belgian urban highways are generally well built and maintained with extensive lighting systems, but rain and fog often reduce visibility. Rural roads are less likely to be illuminated at night. You will find 60 miles of coastline protected by sand dunes and striking beaches, not to mention many quaint resort towns. Travel inland to Bruges, "The Venice of the North," a must see stop-over.

The eastern region of Belgium is home of the Ardennes. Steep river valleys and thickly forested slopes are accented with castles, stone-built villages, and farmhouses. The landscape from River Meuse and on into Luxembourg will leave you speechless.

Forests of mammoth electricity generating windmills dot the countryside, reminiscent of the tales of *Don Quixote*. Ageless small hotels and bed and breakfasts may be found down the least driven roads and atop scenic mountains. Watch carefully; only small roadside signs mark some of the very best accommodations.

FAST FACTS

Area	30,528 Sq. Kilometers or 11,786 Sq. Miles About the size of Maryland
Primary Language	Dutch (Flemish) 60%, French 40%[1]
Nationality	*noun:* Belian(s) *adjective:* Belgian
Currency	Euro (EUR)
Primary Religions	Roman Catholic 75%, Protestant 25%
Population	10,400,000
Capital / Population	Brussels / 981,200
Other Large Cities / Population	Antwerp / 450,000 Ghent / 227,000 Charleori / 202,000 Liege / 186,000 Bruges 117,000

[1] Author's Note: Dutch and Flemish are often used synonymously. The difference between the languages has been compared to the difference between American and British English.

DRIVING FACTS

License	Minimum driving age is 18. Valid U.S. driver license is accepted for stays of less than 90 days.	
Speed Limits *(If not posted)*	Neighborhoods	As posted
	Built up areas	50 kph / 31 mph
	Major roads outside towns	190 kph / 56 mph
	Highways	120 kph / 74 mph
Speed / Distance	Kilometers Per Hour KPH / Meters – Kilometers	
Side of the Road	Drive on the right side of the road unless One-Way	
Roundabouts	Vehicles in the roundabout have the right-of-way over vehicles entering the circle. When in the roundabout, drive in a COUNTER-CLOCKWISE direction.	
Seat Belts	Front Seats	Required
	Rear Seats	Required if available
	Children	• Under 12 years are not allowed in front seat unless in an approved seat or harness
Traffic Lights	As in the U.S., Green means GO and Red means STOP. Yellow signals to STOP until the intersection is cleared of traffic. You may then proceed safely.	
Right on Red	No, unless green arrow is present.	

Required Equipment	Warning triangle	
	Fire extinguisher	
	Helmets are required for motorcycle drivers and passengers	
Pedestrians	Pedestrians and bicyclists have an unconditional right-of-way over vehicles turning left or right. Right-of-way in crosswalks is determined by local signage.	
Tolls	Generally there are no tolls, however, you may encounter a tunnel here and there that does charge to pass through.	
Parking	In most of the larger cities, you must purchase pay for street parking. Vouchers may be obtained from any of several parking kiosks and displayed on your dash or visible through the front window. Carefully check for parking instructional signs wherever you park. Do not park within 15 meters of a tram, bus stop or street car / train tracks.	
Fuel	Unleaded Regular 92 octane	*Normale sans Plomb*
	Unleaded Super 95 octane	*Super sans Plomb*
	Diesel	*Dieselmotor, Diesel*
Motorcycles	Helmets are mandatory	
	Headlights required at all times	
Fines	Law enforcement may collect fines during the traffic stop. Be sure to get an official receipt.	

Drinking and Driving	You will be considered to be impaired and subject to arrest if your BAC is .05% (.5 mg.ml) or more.
Misc.	• Traffic coming from the right generally has priority at uncontrolled intersections and roundabouts, even if coming from a smaller street. • It is a violation to change lanes within an intersection.
U.S. State Department Traffic Safety and Road Conditions[2]	Safety of Public Transportation: Good Urban Road Conditions/Maintenance: Good Rural Road Conditions/Maintenance: Good Availability of Roadside Assistance: Good

EMERGENCY TELEPHONE NUMBERS

Police	101
Fire	100
Ambulance	100
From a Mobile Phone	Dial 112 for any emergency
US Embassy	Regentlaan 27 Boulevard du Régent B-1000 Brussels Tel: +32-2-508-2111 Fax: +32-2-511-2725

[2]Author's Note: I have generally found the State Department's road assessments very accurate, but in the case of Belgium, I disagree wholeheartedly. I found both urban and rural roads to be in excellent condition and easy to navigate.

TERMS OR WORDS YOU MAY SEE ON THE ROAD

English	French	Dutch
Attention	Attention Danger	Let op!
Bed and Breakfast	Chambre d'hôte	Logies en ontbijt
Car	Voiture, véhicule	Auto
Car Rental Agency	Agence de location de voiture	Autoverhuurbedrijf
Caution	Attention Danger	Voorzichtig
Detour	Détour	Wegomleiding
Diesel	Diesel	Diesel
East	Est	Oost
Entrance	Entrée	Oprit
Exit (roadway)	Sortie	Afrit
Expressway	Autoroute, Route Rapide, Rocade, Périphérique	Snelweg
Forbidden	Interdit	Verboden
Gasoline	Essence	Benzine
Hospital	Hôpital	Ziekenhuis
Hotel	Hôtel	Hotel
Left (direction)	Gauche	Links
Motor Oil	Huile de moteur	Motorolie
Museum	Musée	Museum
No Parking	Défense de stationner, Stationnement Interdit	Verboden te Parkeren
North	Nord	Noord
One-way	Sens Unique	Eenrichtingverkeer
Parking	Parking	Parkeren
Parking Lot	Zone de stationnement, Parking	Parkeerplaats
Police	Police	Politie
Police Station	Commissariat, Gendarmerie	Politiebureau
Repeat Sign	Rappel	Rappel
Restaurant	Restaurant	Restaurant
Right (direction)	Droite	Rechts
Road Closed	Route fermée	Weg afgesloten/ geen doorgang
Room for Rent	Chambre á louer	Kamer te huur
Slow	Ralentir	Langzaam Rijden

English	French	Dutch
South	Sud	Zuid
Street	Rue	Straat
Toll Road	Péage	Tolweg
Truck	Camion, poids lourd	Vrachtwagen
Welcome	Bienvenu	Welkom
West	Ouest	West
Yield	Céder le passage	Voorrang verlenen

An excuse you might try if involved in a traffic accident. (According to urban legends, it worked in the U.S.)

L'autre voiture m'a percuté, sans signaler ses intentions de changement de direction."

(Translation: "The other car ran into me without warning me of its intent.")

A great opening line for that awkward moment you absolutely cannot think of a way to start a conversation.

Un escargot peut dormir pendant 3 (trois) ans.

(Translation: "A snail can sleep for three years.")

10 CZECH REPUBLIC

LOCAL SPELLING: *CESKA REPUBLIKA*
ABBREVIATION: CZ

A rare opportunity to witness a newly developing country emerging from its post-Communist era may be found by visiting the Czech Republic. Czechs embrace capitalism, are very friendly and genuinely interested in other cultures. The U.S. State Department rates the crime in the Czech Republic as generally low. Normal caution for pick pockets and muggings in the high tourist area is warned. Music and arts range from classical to the oompah-bands and folk dance.

The Czech Republic is divided into two general regions, Bohemia to the west and Moravia in the east. Moravia leads to the Carpathian Mountains with the prospect of visiting the massive Punkva Caves near Pusty Zleb. Throughout southern Bohemia you will find medieval towns and castles dating back to the 13th century. Another tactic to chart a great driving vacation is to follow the major rivers in search of little villages, towns and vineyards. The Czech Republic certainly provides many such opportunities.

Most tourists automatically gravitate to Prague. If that is your primary target, consider taking a train as you will encounter the same issues as any other large town - dense traffic and little parking. Drive away from the big city and you will find castles, chateaus, historic towns and ancient villages waiting to be discovered. Be sure you begin your search for accommodations early, as there is a shortage of hotels throughout the country (but this is quickly changing). You may see signs indicating *Zimmer frei*. This is a room with breakfast in a private home, an excellent way to meet the people of the Republic.

Auto theft continues to be a problem in the countries that used to be referred to as the "Eastern Block Countries." For this reason, many car rental agencies do not allow their vehicles to cross their borders. In some instances, simply driving across the border is legally sufficient to establish the crime of theft (the guys in the black robes call that *prima facie evidence*). The roads throughout the Czech Republic are generally good and gas stations are easily found.

FAST FACTS

Area	78,866 Sq. Kilometers or 30,450 Sq. Miles Slightly smaller than South Carolina
Primary Language	Czech
Nationality	*noun:* Czech(s) *adjective:* Czech
Currency	Czech koruna (CZK)
Primary Religions	Atheist 40%, Roman Catholic 40%, Protestant 5%
Population	10,200,000
Capital / Population	Prague / 1,400,000
Other Large Cities / Population	Brno / 375,000 Ostrava / 318,000

DRIVING FACTS

License	Minimum driving age is 18. A U.S. driver license must be accompanied by an International Driver's Permit (obtainable in the U.S. from American Automobile Association and the American Automobile Touring Alliance).	
Speed Limits **(If not posted)**	Neighborhoods	As posted
	Built up areas	50 kph / 31 mph
	Major roads outside towns	90 kph / 56 mph
	Highways	130 kph / 80 mph
Speed / Distance	Kilometers Per Hour KPH / Meters – Kilometers	
Side of the Road	Drive on the right side of the road unless One-Way	
Roundabouts	Vehicles in the roundabout have the right-of-way over vehicles entering the circle. When in the roundabout, drive in a COUNTER-CLOCKWISE direction.	
Seat Belts	Front Seats	Required
	Rear Seats	Required if available
	Children	• Under 12 years and less than 1.5 meters are not allowed in front seat • Required for all children under 18 years old and smaller than 4'10"
Traffic Lights	The rules governing traffic lights are the same as in the U.S.	
Right on Red	No	

Required Equipment	Warning triangle First aid kit Extra bulb kits	
Pedestrians	Pedestrians and bicyclists have an unconditional right-of-way over vehicles turning left or right. Right-of-way in crosswalks is determined by local signage.	
Tolls	To travel the major highways, your car must bear a special sticker on the windscreen. Should you rent your car in another country, be sure that they know you will be driving in the Czech Republic and provide you with the proper documentation.	
Parking	In most of the larger cities, you must pay for street parking. Vouchers may be obtained from any of several parking kiosks and displayed on your dash or visible through the front window. Carefully check for parking instructional signs wherever you park.	
Fuel	Unleaded Regular 95/98 octane Diesel	*Benzin Natural* *TT Diesel* or *Nafta*
Motorcycles	Helmets are mandatory Headlights required at all times	
Fines	Law enforcement may collect fines during the traffic stop. Be sure to get an official receipt.	

Drinking and Driving	The Czech Republic has no tolerance for drinking and driving. Any level of alcohol is illegal while driving.
U.S. State Department Traffic Safety and Road Conditions	Safety of Public Transportation: Good Urban Road Conditions/Maintenance: Good Rural Road Conditions/Maintenance: Good Availability of Roadside Assistance: Good

EMERGENCY TELEPHONE NUMBERS

Police	158
Fire	150
Ambulance	155
US Embassy	Trziste 15 118 01 Praha 1 Prague Tel: (+420) 257 530 663

TERMS OR WORDS YOU MAY SEE ON THE ROAD

English	Czech
Attention	Pozor!
Bed and Breakfast	Nocleh se snídaní
Car	Auto
Car Rental Agency	Půjcovna automobilů
Caution	Opatrne
Detour	Objí•ďka
Diesel	Nafta
East	Východ
Entrance	Vchod, Vjezd
Exit (roadway)	Exit, Vyjezd
Expressway	Dálnice
Forbidden	Zakazany
Gasoline	Benzin
Hospital	H Nemocnice
Hotel	Hotel
Left (direction)	doleva, vlevo
Motor Oil	Motorový Olej
Museum	Muzeum
No Parking	Zákaz parkování
North	Sever
One-way	Jednosmerny Provoz
Parking	Parkování
Parking Lot	Parkovište
Passenger Vehicle	Osoloní automobil
Police	Policie
Police Station	Policejní Stanice
Restaurant	Restaurace
Right (direction)	doprava, napravo
Road Closed	Prujezd Zakazan
Room for Rent	Pokoj k pronajmutí
Slow	Pomalu
South	Jih
Street	Ulice
Toll Road	Ddlnice s Mýthrým
Truck	Naklaní automobil
Welcome	Vítejte! Vítat
West	Západ
Yield	Dát prednost

An excuse you might try if involved in a traffic accident. (According to urban legends, it worked in the U.S.)

Vyjela jsem ze strany silnice, podivala se na svou tchyni, a zamirila rovnou do stromu.

(Translation: "I drove away from the side of the road, looked at my mother-in-law and drove into the ditch.")

A great opening line for that awkward moment you absolutely cannot think of a way to start a conversation.

Zena mrka dvakrat vice nez muz.

(Translation: "Women blink almost twice as often as men.")

Translation courtesy of Katerina Prikrylova, General Manager Hotel Ruze

11 DENMARK

LOCAL SPELLING: *DANMARK*
ABBREVIATION: DK

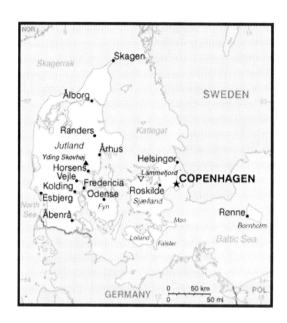

Danish expressways, highways, and secondary roads are of high quality and connect all areas of the country. It is possible to drive from the northern tip of Denmark to the German border in the south in just four hours. Denmark boasts of one of the greatest driving experiences possible, the *Marguerite-ruten* (Marguerite Route), often called "the Daisy Route," aptly taking that name for the signs marking the trail.

The *Marguerite-ruten* is generally a compilation of 2,100 miles of minor roads that are not suitable for buses, trucks or larger vehicles - perfect for tourists in cars and bicycles. It is a circular route following the coast of Denmark and its boarders, with a few roads running east-west and past picturesque villages, hill tops, gardens and 200 of the must see sites of Denmark. These scenic country roads passing through the most beautiful part of Denmark take

you by the same castles and manors a young Hans Christian Anderson spent his formative years before writing such classics as *The Emperor's New Clothes*, *The Little Mermaid* and *The Ugly Duckling*. You may explore the Vikings' history and the Danish Golden Age. On a good day near Skælskør, you may catch a glimpse at the Kanehøj Mill, erected around 1880, one of Denmark's last Dutch windmills; or, the Great Belt Bridge, the world's second largest suspension bridge, connecting Denmark and Zealand.

FAST FACTS

Area	43,094 Sq. Kilometers or 16,638 Sq. Miles Twice the size of New Jersey
Primary Language	Danish, Faroese, Greenlandic, German *Note: English is the predominate second language*
Nationality	*noun:* Dane(s) *adjective:* Danish
Currency	Danish krone (DKK)
Primary Religions	Evangelical Lutheran 95%
Population	5,400,000
Capital / Population	Copenhagen / 1,100,000
Other Large Cities / Population	Arhus / 221,000 Odense / 145,000

DRIVING FACTS

License	Minimum driving age is 18. A valid driver license may be used while visiting Denmark, but the driver must be at least 18 years old.	
Speed Limits *(If not posted)*	Neighborhoods	As posted
	Built up areas	50 kph / 31 mph
	Major roads outside towns	80 kph / 50 mph
	Highways	110 kph / 68 mph
Speed / Distance	Kilometers Per Hour KPH / Meters – Kilometers	
Side of the Road	Drive on the right side of the road unless One-Way	
Roundabouts	Vehicles in the roundabout have the right-of-way over vehicles entering the circle. When in the roundabout, drive in a COUNTER-CLOCKWISE direction.	
Seat Belts	Front Seats	Required
	Rear Seats	Required if available
	Children	• Children under 3 not allowed in front seat except in a child safety seat.
		• In rear seats, children between 3 and 7 must use a child safety seat or booster seat.
Traffic Lights	As in the U.S., <u>Green</u> means GO and <u>Red</u> means STOP. <u>Yellow</u> signals to STOP until the intersection is cleared of traffic. You may then proceed safely. <u>Red+Yellow</u> signal means PREPARE TO GO.	
Right on Red	No, unless green arrow is present.	

Required Equipment	Warning triangle First aid kit and fire extinguishers are recommended.
Pedestrians	Pedestrians and bicyclists have an unconditional right-of-way over vehicles turning left or right. Right-of-way in crosswalks is determined by local signage.
Tolls	There are no toll roads in Denmark.
Parking	In most of the larger cities, you must pay for street parking. Vouchers may be obtained from any of several parking kiosks and displayed on your dash or visible through the front window. Carefully check for parking instructional signs wherever you park.

Fuel	Unleaded Regular 91 octane	*Blyfri Benzin*
	Unleaded Super 95 octane	*Blyfri Benzin-95*
	Diesel	*Diezel*

Motorcycles	Helmets are mandatory
Fines	Law enforcement may collect fines during the traffic stop. Be sure to get an official receipt.

Drinking and Driving	You will be considered to be impaired and subject to arrest if your BAC is .05% (.5 mg.ml) or more.
Misc.	Typically, you must yield to traffic from the right. Right-of-way is usually indicated by a sign with white triangles pointing in the direction of the oncoming vehicle.
U.S. State Department Traffic Safety and Road Conditions	Safety of Public Transportation: Excellent Urban Road Conditions/Maintenance: Excellent Rural Road Conditions/Maintenance: Good Availability of Roadside Assistance: Good

EMERGENCY TELEPHONE NUMBERS

Police	112
Fire	112
Ambulance	112
US Embassy	Dag Hammarskjölds Allé 24 2100 København Ø. Copenhagen Tel. (+45) 35 55 31 44 Fax: (+45) 35 43 02 23

TERMS OR WORDS YOU MAY SEE ON THE ROAD

English	Danish
Attention	Pas på!
Bed and Breakfast	Værelse til leje
Car	Bil
Car Rental Agency	Biludlejning
Caution	Forsigtig kørsel
Detour	Omkørsel
Diesel	Diesel
East	Øst
Entrance	Indkørsel
Exit (roadway)	Udkørsel
Expressway	Motorvej
Forbidden	Forbudt
Gasoline	Benzin
Hospital	Hospital
Hotel	Hotel
Left (direction)	Venstre
Motor Oil	Motorolie
Museum	Museum
No Parking	Parkering forbudt
North	Nord
One-way	Ensrettet færdsel
Parking	Parkering
Parking Lot	Parkeringsplads
Passenger Vehicle	Personbil
Police	Politi
Police Station	Politistation
Restaurant	Restaurant
Right (direction)	Hoejre (højre)
Road Closed	Lukket vej
Room for Rent	Værelse til leje
Slow	Langsom
South	Syd
Street	Gade
Toll Road	Told
Truck	Lastbil
Welcome	Velkommen
West	Vest
Yield	Giv signal

An excuse you might try if involved in a traffic accident. (According to urban legends, it worked in the U.S.)

Jeg troede ikke, at den gamle mand kunne nå over vejen, derfor ramte jeg ham.

(Translation: "I was sure the old man would not make it to the other side of the street so I struck him.")

A great opening line for that awkward moment you absolutely cannot think of a way to start a conversation.

Stort set er de fleste folk mere bange for edderkopper end for døden.

(Translation: "On average, more people fear spiders than death.")

Translation courtesy of Boye Nielsen, Chief Detective, Copenhagen Police

12 FINLAND

LOCAL SPELLING: *SUOMI*
ABBREVIATION: **FI**

Finland is a fairly flat country, seldom rising more than 600 feet above sea level. Although, being in the same latitude as Siberia and Alaska, Finland enjoys a much warmer climate due to the influence of the Gulf Stream.

In the southern region just northeast of Helsinki is the district of Saimaa, often called the "Lake District" where navigable rivers, hundreds of lakes and lakeside villages abound. Finland has managed to keep up with a modern world, yet maintain its true culture and identity.

Drive north, past the Arctic Circle into Lapland and enjoy white water rafting, and hiking up Finland's highest mountain (4,300 feet), Haltitunturi, that is located near the village of Enontekiö. During mid summer, you will find the sun does not set for several weeks.

If driving in the open country is your thing, you will thoroughly enjoy the endless forests, open fields and wide skies. When driving into the rural areas, accommodations and supplies may be at a premium, so ensure your gas tank is full and you have plenty of snacks. Above all, be sure you know where you are going. Saunas are a way of life to the Finns. There are an estimated 1.6 million saunas in Finland, one for every three citizens, and many hotels will have one for your enjoyment. While most are electrically heated, traditional wood heated saunas may be found and are a special treat.

Driving in Finland during the winter months can be hazardous; daylight hours are very short and one should be comfortable with driving in darkness on slick highways. Icy road conditions are common and all vehicles must be equipped with studded snow tires. Many believe that Santa Clause has a time-share somewhere in northern Finland.

Pick your time wisely, check available resources, and you may have an excellent chance at viewing the Aurora Borealis, otherwise known as the Northern Lights. The National Oceanographic and Atmospheric Administration's (NOAA) Space Environment Center web page (**http://www.sec.noaa.gov/index.html**) is an excellent resource for determining the best times to view the Northern Lights.

Winter or summer, when driving at night in rural areas, drivers must be alert to reindeer and moose wandering onto the roadways. There have been incidents of moose being struck by vehicles, causing severe damage to the vehicle and injury, sometimes fatal, to the occupants.

FAST FACTS

Area	337,030 Sq. Kilometers or 130,128 Sq. Miles Slightly smaller than Montana
Primary Language	Finnish 93%, Swede 6%
Nationality	*noun:* Finn(s) *adjective:* Finnish
Currency	Euro (EUR)
Primary Religions	Evangelical Lutheran 89%, none 9%
Population	5,100,111
Capital / Population	Helsinki / 1,200,000
Other Large Cities / Population	Espoo / 230,000 Tampere / 201,000

DRIVING FACTS

License	Minimum driving age is 18. A valid driver license must be accompanied with your passport.
Speed Limits *(If not posted)*	Neighborhoods — As posted Built up areas — 30-50 kph / 19-31 mph Major roads outside towns — 80-100 kph / 50-62 mph Highways — 120-130 kph / 75-80 mph
Speed / Distance	Kilometers Per Hour KPH / Meters – Kilometers
Side of the Road	Drive on the right side of the road unless One-Way
Roundabouts	Vehicles in the roundabout have the right-of-way over vehicles entering the circle. When in the roundabout, drive in a COUNTER-CLOCKWISE direction.
Seat Belts	Front Seats — Required Rear Seats — Required if available Children — • Under 12 years and less than 1.5 meters are not allowed in front seat unless in an approved seat or harness • Under 12 but over 1.5 meters must use adult belt
Traffic Lights	As in the U.S., Green means GO and Red means STOP. Yellow signals to STOP until the intersection is cleared of traffic. You may then proceed safely. Red+Yellow signal means PREPARE TO GO.
Right on Red	No, unless green arrow is present.

Required Equipment	Warning triangle
	First aid kit, extra bulb kits and fire extinguishers are recommended.
Pedestrians	Pedestrians and bicyclists have an unconditional right-of-way over vehicles turning left or right. Right-of-way in crosswalks is determined by local signage.
Tolls	There are no tolls in Finland.
Parking	Parking lights must be used if in dimly lit public areas. Vehicles may be towed/impounded for illegal parking violations.

Fuel		
	Unleaded Regular 91 octane	*Lyijytoen*
	Unleaded Super 95 octane	*Lyijytoen*
	Diesel	*Diesel*

Motorcycles	Helmets are mandatory
Fines	Police are not empowered to collect fines on the spot. Fines must be paid at banks and post offices. The minimum fine is €130 and there is no maximum limit.

Drinking and Driving	You will be considered to be impaired and subject to arrest if your BAC is .05% (.5 mg.ml) or more.
Misc.	• Headlights must be used at all times. • Use of horns in towns and villages is illegal except for emergencies. • It is a violation to change lanes within an intersection.
U.S. State Department Traffic Safety and Road Conditions	Safety of Public Transportation: Excellent Urban Road Conditions/Maintenance: Excellent Rural Road Conditions/Maintenance: Excellent Availability of Roadside Assistance: Excellent

EMERGENCY TELEPHONE NUMBERS

Police	112
Fire	112
Ambulance	112
US Embassy	Itäinen Puistotie 14 B FIN-00140 Helsinki Tel: +358-9-616 250

TERMS OR WORDS YOU MAY SEE ON THE ROAD

English	Finnish
Attention	Huomio
Bed and Breakfast	Aamiaismajoitus
Car	Auto
Caution	Varo
Detour	Kiertotie
Diesel	Diesel
East	Itä
Entrance	Sisääntulo
Exit (roadway)	Ulosajo
Forbidden	Kielletty
Gasoline	Polttoaine
Expressway	Moottoritie
Hospital	Sairaala
Hotel	Hotelli
Left (direction)	Vasen
Motor Oil	Moottoriöljy
Museum	Museo
No Parking	Paikoitus kielletty
North	Pohjoinen
One-way	Yksisuuntainen
Parking	Paikoitus
Parking Lot	Paikoitusalue
Passenger Vehicle	Henkilöauto
Police	Poliisi
Police Station	Poliisiasema
Car Rental Agency	Autovuokraamo
Restaurant	Ravintola
Right (direction)	Oikea
Road Closed	Tie suljettu
Room for Rent	Vuokrattavia huoneita
Slow	Hidas
South	Etelä
Street	Katu
Toll Road	Maksullinen tie
Truck	Kuorma-auto
Welcome	Tervetuloa
West	Länsi
Yield	Etuajo-oikeus

An excuse you might try if involved in a traffic accident. (According to urban legends, it worked in the U.S.)

Olin ajanut autoani neljäkymmentä vuotta kun nukahdin ja jouduin onnettomuuteen.

(Translation: "I had been driving my car for forty years when I fell asleep at the wheel and had an accident.")

A great opening line for that awkward moment you absolutely cannot think of a way to start a conversation.

Sähkötuoli oli hammaslääkärin keksimä.

(Translation: "The electric chair was invented by a dentist.")

Translation courtesy ofof Liisa Kujanpää, American Embassy Helsinki

13 FRANCE

LOCAL SPELLING: *FRANCE*
ABBREVIATION: FR

Driving into larger French cities can be daunting at best. The French are notorious for their aggressive and inconsiderate driving habits.

The largest country in Western Europe, France offers a very diverse landscape. The rolling planes of north-central France, dense forests in the Argon Valley, majestic Alpine mountains and seascape of every description on both the Atlantic Ocean and Mediterranean coasts, offer a traveler limitless experiences.

One of the most common vacation themes in France is to follow the vineyard roads, which are plentiful throughout the country. Whether you are seeking the Rieslings of Alsace in the northeast, Loire wines in the central region or the reds in southwest Bordeaux, the common thread you will find are scenic highways, quaint villages, excellent food and nice people. France is rich with history. Should tracking history excite you, you can may retrace our fathers' footsteps during the World Wars, follow the path of the Roman Armies, or follow any one of many religious routes.

La Route des Cretes in the Alsaece-Lorraine region offers richly forested mountains, and resembles Germany's Black Forest, and runs adjacent to the western edge of the Rhine River. Nearby, from Colmar, you may pick up the wine road, the *Route du Vin*, which strings together family wineries, quaint villages, and feudal fortresses. Further south on the eastern side of France lies *La Route des Grandes Alpes*, running approximately 450 miles through Morine, Chamonix and Megeve. The road is one of the most panoramic drives in western Europe, passing through Alpine uplands, large forests, glaciers and Alpine foothills.

While there is an endless selection of novels written in a French setting, you may find *The DaVinci Code* intriguing if you are in or near Paris, and especially a good read if you are doing an England-France vacation.

On the major highways, service stations are situated at least every 25 miles. When venturing into the countryside, you may have a harder time finding gas. Never let your gas gauge go beyond half full, and you should have no problems.

Authors Note: Just a quick word about the post 9-11 French. I have been told that I am patriotic *ad nauseam* and, quite frankly, I was little reluctant to travel into France after the attacks on September 11, 2001. As my wife and I traveled through France's countryside, we approached the people we met with a little trepidation and I suspect they felt the same. We greeted each one with a smile and tried (usually ineffectively) to communicate in their language. Our overtures were met in kind and we found most of the French people we met to be friendly, polite and helpful. The personal emotions that well up when standing on the hallowed ground where our fathers and grandfathers fought, died and are buried are too important to miss because the politicians got catty-whompus with each other. There are 24 permanent American burial grounds on foreign soil that hold 124,917 of our war dead. Eleven of these cemeteries are in France. If for no other reason, our pilgrimages to France must continue; we must never abandon those brave souls. You may find additional information about our American war dead buried on foreign ground on the internet at **http://www.abmc.gov/abmc2.htm**.

FAST FACTS

Area	547,030 Sq. Kilometers or 211,209 Sq. Miles Slightly less than the size of Texas
Primary Language	French
Nationality	*noun:* Frenchman (men), Frenchwoman (women) *adjective:* French
Currency	Euro (EUR)
Primary Religions	Roman Catholic 83-88%, Muslim 5-10%
Population	50,400,000
Capital / Population	Paris / 11,300,000
Other Large Cities / Population	Marseille / 821,000 Lyon / 444,000 Toulouse / 412,000 Nice / 332,000 Nantes / 282,000 Strasbourg / 272,000 Bordeaux / 217,000

DRIVING FACTS

License	Minimum driving age is 18. A valid driver license must be accompanied with your passport.

Speed Limits **(If not posted)**	Neighborhoods	As posted
	Built up areas	50 kph / 31 mph
	Major roads outside towns	90 kph / 56 mph
	Highways	110 kph / 68 mph
	Highways	130 kph / 80 mph

Speed / Distance	Kilometers Per Hour KPH / Meters – Kilometers
Side of the Road	Drive on the right side of the road unless One-Way
Roundabouts	Vehicles in the roundabout have the right-of-way over vehicles entering the circle. When in the roundabout, drive in a COUNTER-CLOCKWISE direction.

Seat Belts	Front Seats	Required
	Rear Seats	Required if available
	Children	• Under 10 years must be in the rear using an approved child seat or safety harness
		• Infants to 9 months may be in the front seat is in an approved, rear facing seat

Traffic Lights	As in the U.S., Green means GO and Red means STOP. Orange signals to STOP until the intersection is cleared of traffic. You may then proceed safely.
Right on Red	No, unless green arrow is present.

Required Equipment	Warning triangle First aid kit Extra bulb kits and fire extinguishers are recommended.	
Pedestrians	Pedestrians and bicyclists have an unconditional right-of-way over vehicles turning left or right. Right-of-way in crosswalks is determined by local signage.	
Tolls	Tolls are levied on most highways (autoroutes).	
Parking	In most of the larger cities, you must pay for street parking. Vouchers may be obtained from any of several parking kiosks and displayed on your dash or visible through the front window. Carefully check for parking instructional signs wherever you park.	
Fuel	Unleaded Regular 95/98 octane Diesel	*Essance sans Plomb* *Gazole or Gas-oil or Gaz-oil*
Motorcycles	Helmets are mandatory Headlights required at all times	
Fines	Law enforcement may collect fines during the traffic stop. Be sure to get an official receipt.	

Drinking and Driving	You will be considered to be impaired and subject to arrest if your BAC is .05% (.5 mg.ml) or more.
Misc.	Some car rental agencies have strict policies forbidding travel into countries bordering Austria's eastern and southern borders. Simply crossing the border in some locations may be considered auto theft. Even if it is an honest mistake or simple error in judgment, the cost and incontinence may be monumental. Read your contract and abide by the conditions.
U.S. State Department Traffic Safety and Road Conditions	Safety of Public Transportation: Good Urban Road Conditions/Maintenance: Good Rural Road Conditions/Maintenance: Good Availability of Roadside Assistance: Good

EMERGENCY TELEPHONE NUMBERS

Police	17
Fire	18
Ambulance	15
US Embassy	2 Avenue Gabriel 75008 Paris Tel: 33 1 43 12 22 22

TERMS OR WORDS YOU MAY SEE ON THE ROAD

English	French
Attention	Attention Danger
Bed and Breakfast	Chambre d'hôte
Car	Voiture, véhicule
Caution	Attention Danger
Detour	Détour
Diesel	Diesel
East	Est
Entrance	Entrée
Exit (roadway)	Sortie
Expressway	Autoroute, Route Rapide, Rocade, Périphérique
Forbidden	Interdit
Gasoline	Essence
Hospital	Hôpital
Hotel	Hôtel
Left (direction)	Gauche
Motor Oil	Huile de moteur
Museum	Musée
No Parking	Défense de stationner, Stationnement Interdit
North	Nord
One-way	Sens Unique
Parking	Parking
Parking Lot	Zone de stationnement, Parking
Passenger Vehicle	Voiture de tourisme
Police	Police
Police Station	Commissariat, Gendarmerie
Repeat Sign	Rappel
Restaurant	Restaurant
Right (direction)	Droite
Road Closed	Route fermée
Room for Rent	Chambre á louer
Slow	Ralentir
South	Sud
Street	Rue
Toll Road	Péage
Truck	Camion, poids lourd
Welcome	Bienvenu
West	Ouest
Yield	Céder le passage

An excuse you might try if involved in a traffic accident. (According to urban legends, it worked in the U.S.)

L'autre voiture est entrée en collision avec la mienne sans avoir prévenu de ses intentions.

(Translation: "The other car collided with mine without giving warning of its intentions.")

A great opening line for that awkward moment you absolutely cannot think of a way to start a conversation.

Un crocodile ne peut pas sortir sa langue.

(Translation: "A crocodile cannot stick its tongue out.")

Translation courtesy of Auger Thierry, French Police, Antibes, France

14 GERMANY

LOCAL SPELLING: *DEUTSCHLAND*
ABBREVIATION: DE

Home of the first super highway, Germany's Autobahn will take you from the valleys and river basins of the North German Plains to the heights of Bavaria. While most people travel at speeds common to the other European highways, there is no speed limit. The Germans' right to speed is a closely guarded right. If you feel the urge for speed, this is the place; but be sure your vehicle is up to the task and you do not drive beyond your capabilities. Get off the Autobahn and you will find a secondary road system that is...second to none. Along the way are countless towns and villages that seem to jump out of travel books and children's fairy tales. It seems as if every hilltop is capped with a castle, some abandoned and some in use, some owned privately while others are open to the public. Enchanting hotels, excellent restaurants, cafés and interesting sights are just around every turn.

Generally, road conditions in western Germany are excellent. You should be a little more cautious while traveling on older roads in eastern Germany. The high speed permitted on the German Autobahn, unfamiliar road markings and those cold German winters may pose considerable hazards. Driver error is the number one cause of accidents involving American driving tourists in Germany.

The *Romantische Strasse* or Romantic Road, runs from Wurzburg to Füssen, and will take you through Germany's most beautiful rural terrain, by well preserved thousand-year-old walled towns and castles. If you are a Brothers Grimm fan, you will not want to miss the *Fairy Tale Road* which runs from Hanau (home of the Grimm Brothers) to Bremen and is where Little Red Riding Hood, Sleeping Beauty and many others originated. There is also the *Castle Road*, a 365-mile castle-hopping journey from Heidelberg and Nürnburg that takes in many medieval towns including Rothenburg, Heidleberg and Neuschwanstein (the inspiration for Cinderella's castle at Disneyland and Disney World). There are approximately 80 themed highways in Germany to be explored.

FAST FACTS

Area	357,021 Sq. Kilometers or 137,846 Sq. Miles Slightly smaller than Montana
Primary Language	German
Nationality	*noun:* German(s) *adjective:* German
Currency	Euro (EUR)
Primary Religions	Protestant 34%, Roman Catholic 34%, Muslim 4%
Population	82,500,000
Capital / Population	Berlin / 4,000,000
Other Large Cities / Population	Hamburg / 1,700,000 Munich / 1,185,000 Cologne / 965,000 Frankfurt / 648,000

DRIVING FACTS

License	Minimum driving age is 18 Individuals holding a U.S. driver's license may drive up to 6 months without acquiring a German driver's license.	
Speed Limits **(If not posted)**	Built up areas	50 kph / 31 mph
	Major roads outside towns	100 kph / 62 mph
	Highways (Autobahn)	No Speed Limits
	A note about driving on the Autobahn: Always drive on the right side of the roadway except when passing. Pass, then move quickly back to the right lane. There may be vehicles approaching from behind you at extraordinary speeds. It is in poor fashion in Germany to ride the left lane.	
Speed / Distance	Kilometers Per Hour KPH / Meters – Kilometers	
Side of the Road	Drive on the right side of the road unless One-Way	
Roundabouts	Vehicles in the roundabout have the right-of-way over vehicles entering the circle. When in the roundabout, drive in a COUNTER-CLOCKWISE direction.	
Seat Belts	Front Seats	Required
	Rear Seats	Required if available
	Children	Children under 12 years and less 4'8" must be in the rear seat unless using a child approved seat
Traffic Lights	As in the U.S., Green means GO and Red means STOP. A short Yellow signal means PREPARE TO GO.	
Right on Red	No, unless green arrow is present.	

Required Equipment	Warning triangle First aid kit Extra bulb kit Fire extinguishers	
Pedestrians	Pedestrians and bicyclists have an unconditional right-of-way over vehicles turning left or right. Right-of-way in crosswalks is determined by local signage.	
Tolls	There are no tolls in Germany.	
Parking	Blue Zone rules apply. In most of the larger cities, you must pay for street parking. Vouchers may be obtained from any of several parking kiosks and displayed on your dash or visible through the front window. Carefully check for parking instructional signs wherever you park.	
Fuel	Unleaded Regular 91 octane Unleaded Super 95 octane Unleaded Super 98 octane Diesel	*Bleifrei Normal* *Bleifrei Super* *Bleifrei Super Plus* *Diesel*
Motorcycles	Helmets are mandatory Headlights required at all times	
Fines	Law enforcement may collect fines during the traffic stop. Be sure to get an official receipt.	

Drinking and Driving	You will be considered to be impaired and subject to arrest if your BAC is .05% (.5 mg.ml) or more.
Misc.	Traffic cameras are very common throughout the country. They may be in unmarked police cars or mounted permanently to a bridge or light pole; either way, if you are the subject of a snapshot, expect a notice of fine within a few days. Rental companies will forward notices to the person who was renting their car the date of the infraction.
U.S. State Department Traffic Safety and Road Conditions	Safety of Public Transportation: Excellent Urban Road Conditions/Maintenance: Excellent Rural Road Conditions/Maintenance: Excellent Availability of Roadside Assistance: Excellent

EMERGENCY TELEPHONE NUMBERS

Police	110
Fire	112
Ambulance	115
US Embassy	Neustädtische Kirchstr. 4-5 10117 Berlin Telephone: (030) 8305-0

TERMS OR WORDS YOU MAY SEE ON THE ROAD

English	German
Attention	Achtung
Bed and Breakfast	Gasthaus
Car	Auto
Car Rental Agency	Autovermietung
Caution	Vorsicht
Detour	Umleitung
Diesel	Diesel
East	Osten
Entrance	Eingang / Einfahrt
Exit (roadway)	Ausfahrt
Expressway	Autobahn
Forbidden	Verboten
Gasoline	Benzin
Hospital	Krankenhaus
Hotel	Hotel
Left (direction)	Links
Motor Oil	Motoröl
Museum	Museum
No Parking	Parken verboten
North	Norden
One-way	Einbahnstraße
Parking	Parken
Parking Lot	Parkplatz
Passenger Vehicle	Pkw, Personenwagen
Police	Polizei
Police Station	Polizeistation
Restaurant	Restaurant
Right (direction)	Rechts
Road Closed	Straße gesperrt
Room for Rent	Zimmer zu vermieten
Slow	Geschwindigkeit drosseln / Fahren sie langsamer
South	Süden
Street	Straße (strasse)
Toll Road	Mautstraße
Truck	Lkw, Lastwagen
Welcome	Wilkommen
West	Westen
Yield	Vorfahrt beachten

An excuse you might try if involved in a traffic accident. (According to urban legends, it worked in the U.S.)

Auf dem Weg nach hause habe ich die falsche Einfahrt genommen und bin gegen einen Baum gefahren, den ich zuhause nicht habe.

(Translation: "On my way home, I drove into the wrong house and smashed into a tree I do not have.")

A great opening line for that awkward moment you absolutely cannot think of a way to start a conversation.

Ein Nieser kommt aus dem Mund mit einer Geschwindigkeit vin 161 km/stunde.

(Translation: "A sneeze travels out your mouth at over 100 m.p.h.!")

Translations courtesy of Ursula Alvarez

15 GREECE

LOCAL SPELLING: *ELLAS* OR *ELLADA*
ABBREVIATION: GR

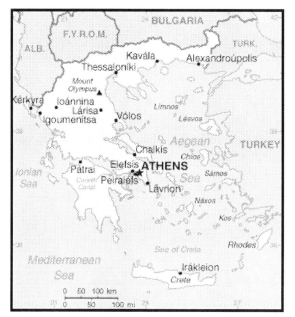

Greece is predominately a rocky and mountainous country, rich with vineyards, olive orchards, and an explosion of wildflowers in the spring. Miles of rocky coastline provide scenic beauty second to none, with many quaint and historic villages.

Here you can walk in the footsteps of early Christianity or explore Greek mythology firsthand. The Olympic games have impacted world history since they began in 776 B.C., and the 2004 Olympics hosted in Greece continued the tradition. The Acropolis rises majestically above the Athens horizon and is bathed in floodlights, creating a breathtaking and memorable sight.

Athens is extremely hot during the summer months, making this a great destination for the spring, fall or winter seasons. In Athens, shorts and bare shoulders are considered poor taste. The Greek alphabet is quite overwhelming, but don't worry, street signs throughout the country are written in both Greek and Roman script.

The Vikos Gorge, one of the most spectacular chasms in Europe, offers nearly 50 small villages conjoined by narrow, windy roads and lined with stunning terrain. Greeks and other Europeans routinely escape to this undeveloped corner of northwestern Greece, yet it still manages to elude the congestion found elsewhere in the country.

If your plans include driving a rental car through several countries on the way to Greece, read your rental contracts carefully. The borders of Greece and Turkey are surrounded by what used to be called the "Eastern Block Countries." Most auto rental contracts prohibit entering those countries. Simply crossing the border into one of the forbidden countries may lead to a quagmire of legal problems. Your best alternative may be to arrive in Greece by air/train/boat and rent a car there.

When driving in Greece, remember the words of your high school driving instructor, "Drive Defensively!" Heavy traffic and poor highway conditions increase the risk to drivers and pedestrians, especially at night. Most of American tourist traffic casualties in Greece were drivers or riders of motorbikes. Greece leads the European Union in motorcycle deaths.

FAST FACTS

Area	131,940 Sq. Kilometers or 50,942 Sq. Miles Slightly smaller than Louisiana
Primary Language	Greek
Nationality	*noun:* Greek(s) *adjective:* Greek
Currency	Euro (EUR)
Primary Religions	Greek Orthodox 98%
Population	10,650,000
Capital / Population	Athens / 3,247,000
Other Large Cities / Population	Thessaloniki / 361,000 Piraeus / 179,000 Patras / 167,000

DRIVING FACTS

License	Minimum driving age is 18. Drivers must carry a valid driver license as well as an International Driver's Permit (IDP). Failure to have both documents may result in police detention or other problems.	
Speed Limits *(If not posted)*	Built up areas	50 kph / 31 mph
	Major roads outside towns	110 kph / 68 mph
	Highways	120 kph / 74 mph
Speed / Distance	Kilometers Per Hour KPH / Meters – Kilometers	
Side of the Road	Drive on the right side of the road unless One-Way	
Roundabouts	Vehicles <u>entering</u> the roundabout have the right-of-way over vehicles in the circle. When in the roundabout, drive in a COUNTER-CLOCKWISE direction.	
Seat Belts	Front Seats	Required
	Rear Seats	Required if available
	Children	Children under the age of 10 are not permitted in the front seat.
Traffic Lights	As in the U.S., <u>Green</u> means GO and <u>Red</u> means STOP. <u>Yellow</u> signals to STOP until the intersection is cleared of traffic. You may then proceed safely.	
Right on Red	No, unless green arrow is present.	

Required Equipment	Warning triangle
	First aid kit
	Extra bulb kits
	Fire extinguisher

Pedestrians	Pedestrians and bicyclists have an unconditional right-of-way over vehicles turning left or right. Right-of-way in crosswalks is determined by local signage.

Tolls	There are no tolls for the public roadways in Greece.

Parking	Parking meters may be found in Athens. No parking within 3 meters of a fire hydrant, 5 meters of an intersection or 15 meters of a bus stop. Police may confiscate your vehicle license plate if your car is found parked in certain No Parking Zones.

Fuel	Unleaded Regular 95/98 octane	*Amolivi*
		vensina
	Diesel	*Diesel*

Motorcycles	Helmets are mandatory

Fines	Unlike most European countries, the police may not collect fines on the spot. Send any applicable fines to the Public Treasury.

Drinking and Driving	You will be considered to be impaired and subject to arrest if your BAC is .05% (.5 mg.ml) or more.
Misc.	It is a violation to change lanes within an intersection.
U.S. State Department Traffic Safety and Road Conditions	Safety of Public Transportation: Good Urban Road Conditions/Maintenance: Good Rural Road Conditions/Maintenance: Fair Availability of Roadside Assistance: Fair and improving

EMERGENCY TELEPHONE NUMBERS

Police	100
Fire	199
Ambulance	166
Roadside Assistance	10400
US Embassy	91 Vasilissis Sophias Avenue Athens 10160 Tel: 30-210-721-2951

TERMS OR WORDS YOU MAY SEE ON THE ROAD

English	Greek (Greek)	Greek (Roman)
Attention	Προσοχή	Prosohee
Bed and Breakfast	Κρέβάτι και Πρωινό	Krevati ke Proeno
Bus	Λεωφορείο	Leoforio
Bus Station	ΚΤΕΛ	Hktel
Car	Αυτοκίνητο	aftokinito
Car Rental Agency	Ενοικιαζόμενα αυτοκινητα	Enikiazomena Aftokinita
Caution	Προσοχή	Prosohee
Detour	Προσοχή	Parakambses
Diesel	Πετρέλεαιο	Petreleo
East	Ανατολή	Anatolee
Entrance	Είσοδος	Esodos
Exit (roadway)	Εξοδος	Exodos
Expressway	Κεντρικός Δρόμος	Kendrikos Thromos
Forbidden	Απαγορεύεται	Apagorevete
Gasoline	Αμόλυβδχ Βενζίνα	Amolyvdee venzini
Hospital	Νοσοκομείο	Nosokomio
Hotel	Ξενοδοχείο	Ksedonohio
Left (direction)	Αριστερά	Aristera
Motor Oil	Λαδί Μηχανής	Ladi Mihanis
Museum	Μουσείο	Mousio
No Parking	Απαγορεύεται το Παρκάρισμα	Apagorevetai to Parlarosma
North	βοράς	Voras
One-way	Μονόδρομς	Monodromos
Parking Lot	Παρκιν	Parking
Police	Αστιυνομία	Astinomia
Police Station	Αστιυνομίκο Σταθμό / Θύμα	Astinomiko Sthmoa / thima
Restaurant	Εστιατόριο	Estiatorio
Right (direction)	Δεξια	Deksia
Road Closed	Δρόμος Κλειστός	Dromos Klestos
Room for Rent	Ενοικιζόμενα	Enikiazomena
Slow	Σιγά	Siga
South	Νότος	Notos
Street	Δρόμος	Dromos Klestos
Tavern	Ταβέρνα	Taverna
Toll Road	Διόδια	Diodia
Truck	Νταλίκα or Φορτηγο	Dtalika or Fortigo
Welcome	Καλώς ήρθατε	Kalos Erthate
West	Ανατολικού	Anatolikou
Yield	Δινω Προτεραιοιτα	Dino Protereotita

An excuse you might try if involved in a traffic accident. (According to urban legends, it worked in the U.S.)

Eno koimomoun to aytokinhto mou bike se en a ktiro.

(Translation: "While I was sleeping my automobile drove into the building.")

A great opening line for that awkward moment you absolutely cannot think of a way to start a conversation.

Oles oi polices arkoudes, einai aristerohires.

(Translation: "All polar bears are left handed.")

Translation courtesy of Kyriakos Karkalis, International Police Asssociation, Greece

16 HUNGARY

LOCAL SPELLING: *MAGYARORSZÁG*
ABBREVIATION: HU

Should you drive into Hungary from Austria, you will surely find strong ties to the western world, dotted with historic towns and villages surrounded by productive farmlands. Lake Balaton, Hungary's largest lake and number one tourist attraction is rimmed with quaint villages. Mineral springs along the northwest shoreline are a haven for folks with circulatory ailments. Tracing the Danube River running north to south through Budapest is another sure-fire method of

finding the peace and tranquility of old Europe. Drive to the north and you may discover heavily forested hills and vineyards or go south to the Great Plan (*Puszta*).

Be sure to carefully read your car rental agreement prior to driving your rental car into Hungary from another country. An innocent, errant border crossing may result in lengthy and unpleasant conversations with a Polish *rendőr* (police officer). Hungarian motorways and highways are generally in good condition. Urban roads and road maintenance are also good. In rural areas, however, roads are often narrow, badly lit, and can be in a state of poor repair in some areas.

FAST FACTS

Area	93,030 Sq. Kilometers or 35,919 Sq. Miles Slightly smaller than Indiana
Primary Language	Hungarian
Nationality	*noun:* Hungarian(s) *adjective:* Hungarian
Currency	Forint (HUF)
Primary Religions	Roman Catholic 67%, Calvinist 20%
Population	10,000,000
Capital / Population	Budapest 2,600,000
Other Large Cities / Population	Debrecen / 210,000 Miskolc / 182,000 Szeged / 173,000

DRIVING FACTS

License	Minimum driving age is 18. Hungary recognizes International Driver's Permits (IDP) issued by the American Automobile Association (AAA) and the American Automobile Touring Alliance when presented with a state driver license. American driver's license will be accepted in Hungary for one year after arrival, provided that a certified Hungarian translation has been attached to the license. Those with IDPs do not need to have the license translated, but must present both IDP and a valid driver license together.	
Speed Limits **(If not posted)**	Neighborhoods	As posted
	Built up areas	50 kph / 31 mph
	Major roads outside towns	100 kph / 62 mph
	Highways	120 kph / 75 mph
Speed / Distance	Kilometers Per Hour KPH / Meters – Kilometers	
Side of the Road	Drive on the right side of the road unless One-Way	
Roundabouts	Vehicles in the roundabout have the right-of-way over vehicles entering the circle. When in the roundabout, drive in a COUNTER-CLOCKWISE direction.	
Seat Belts	Front Seats	Required
	Rear Seats	Required if available
	Children	• Children under 12 or under 4'6" feet tall are not allowed in front seats
		• Children under 4 feet tall or younger than 12 years must use an approved child seat
Traffic Lights	The rules are the same as in the U.S.	
Right on Red	No	

Required Equipment	Warning triangle
	First aid kit
	Extra bulb kit

Pedestrians	Pedestrians and bicyclists have an unconditional right-of-way over vehicles turning left or right. Right-of-way in crosswalks is determined by local signage.

Tolls	There are no tolls on the Hungarian roadways

Parking	Parking is generally acceptable on the roadside, but be sure to face the direction of travel. The Budapest city center is closed to traffic.

Fuel	Unleaded Regular 91 octane	Olommentes uzemanyag 91
	Unleaded Super 95/98 octane	Olommentes uzemanyag
	Diesel	Diesel

Motorcycles	Helmets are mandatory
	Headlights required at all times

Fines	Law enforcement may not collect fines during the traffic stop. Fines may be paid at local post offices.

Drinking and Driving	Hungary has no tolerance for drinking and driving. Any level of alcohol in your bloodstream is unlawful.
U.S. State Department Traffic Safety and Road Conditions	Safety of Public Transportation: Good Urban Road Conditions/Maintenance: Good Rural Road Conditions/Maintenance: Fair Availability of Roadside Assistance: Good

EMERGENCY TELEPHONE NUMBERS

Police	107
Fire	105
Ambulance	104
Breakdown	General: 153 4700 or 143 4704 In Budapest: 252 8000
Mobile Phone	Dial 112 for all services
US Embassy	Szabadság tér 12., H-1054 Budapest Tel: (36-1) 475-4400; Fax: (36-1) 475-4764

TERMS OR WORDS YOU MAY SEE ON THE ROAD

English	Hungarian
Attention	Figyelem
Car	Autó
Car Rental Agency	Autókölscönző, autóbérlés
Caution	Veszély
Detour	Kerülőút
Diesel	Gázolaj, Dízel
East	Kelet
Entrance	Bejárat
Exit (roadway)	Kijárat
Expressway	Autópáya, gyorsforgalmi út
Forbidden	Tilos
Gasoline	Benzin
Hospital	Kórhház
Hotel	Hotel, szálloda
Left (direction)	Bal
Motor Oil	Olaj, motorolaj
Museum	Múzeum
No Parking	Parkolni/várakozni tilos, Tilos a parkolás
North	Észak
One-way	Egyirányú
Parking	Parkolás
Parking Lot	Parkoló
Passenger Vehicle	Személygépkocsi, SZGK, személyautó
Police Officer	Rendőr
Police Station	Rendőrség
Restaurant	Etterem, vendéglő, csárda
Right (direction)	Jobb
Road Closed	Utlezárás
Room for Rent	Kiadó szoba, Szoba Kiadó
Slow	Lassú
South	Dél
Street	Út, utca
Toll Road	Fizetős autópálya
Truck	Kamion, teherautó
Welcome	Isten hozta
West	Nyugat
Yield	Elsőbbségadás

An excuse you might try if involved in a traffic accident. (According to urban legends, it worked in the U.S.)

A rendőröknek azt mondtam, hogy nem sebesültem meg, deamikor levettem a kalapom, kiderült, hogy koponyatörésem van.

(Translation: "I told the police that I was not injured, but when I removed my hat, I found that I had a skull fracture.")

A great opening line for that awkward moment you absolutely cannot think of a way to start a conversation.

Szemeink születésünktől fogva ugyanakkorák, de orrunk és fülünk velünk nőnek.

(Translation: "Our eyes are always the same size from birth, but our nose and ears never stop growing.")

Translation courtesy of the Hungarian Embassy in Washington D.C.

17 IRELAND

LOCAL SPELLING: *IRELAND*
ABBREVIATION: IE

A quick geography lesson. Northern Ireland is a providence of the United Kingdom. Ireland is a sovereign government, having declared independence from the United Kingdom in 1921 and withdrew from the British Commonwealth in 1948.

Driving in Ireland is certainly a test of anyone's abilities with narrow lanes and fast drivers everywhere. In the southwestern part of the country, The Lakes of Killarney offer some of the most splendid sights in Ireland, surrounded by magnificent mountains streaked with those little windy roads we all love to drive. The Gulf Stream delivers many surprises along the western coastal roads, such as tropical plants and even coconut trees. Killarney Town has numerous places for the tired traveler including hotels, guesthouses, B&B's and pubs, lots and lots of pubs.

The River Shannon separates east from west, and offers 200 miles of opportunities for the avid driver and tourist seeking natural lands, stunning scenery and quaint villages.

Of course, no trip to Ireland would be complete without kissing the world famous Blarney Stone situated high up in the battlements of the Blarney castle in the southern tip if Ireland. And, on the topic of castles, they are plentiful throughout the country.

Gaelic-Irish is the Official language of Ireland; however, English is commonly spoken throughout the country. Road signs are in both languages, except for areas on the western coast. In an effort to preserve the Gaelic language, in early 2005 the English language was officially removed from road signs affecting more than 2,300 towns, villages and crossroads. Signs once posted in English and Gaelic are now strictly Irish.

Fast Facts

Area	70,280 Sq. Kilometers or 27,135 Sq. Miles Slightly larger than West Virginia
Primary Language	English, Irish (Gaelic) is spoken in some areas
Nationality	*noun:* Irishman(men), Irishwoman(men) *adjective:* Irish
Currency	Euro (EUR)
Primary Religions	Roman Catholic 92%, Church of Ireland 3%
Population	4,000,000
Capital / Population	Dublin / 1,000,000
Other Large Cities / Population	Cork / 193,000 Limerick / 85,000 Galway / 67,000

DRIVING FACTS

License	Minimum driving age is 17. A valid driver license must be accompanied with your passport.	
Speed Limits **(If not posted)**	Built up areas	50 kph / 30 mph
	Major roads outside towns	80-100 kph / 50-60 mph
	Highways	130 kph / 80 mph
Speed / Distance	Officially, Ireland has adopted the metric system of measurement. Like the U.S., Ireland adopted the Imperial System of measurement from Britain and metrics are the only form of measurement taught in schools. Change often comes hard, and the people of Ireland still cling to the old ways. Speed limit signs and distance signs are supposed to be changed during the year 2005, but you will surely find some of the older signs in the rural areas.	
Side of the Road	Drive on the LEFT side of the road unless One-Way	
Roundabouts	Vehicles in the roundabout have the right-of-way over vehicles entering the circle. Don't forget, when entering a roundabout here, be sure to drive in a CLOCKWISE direction.	
Seat Belts	Front Seats	Required
	Rear Seats	Required if available
	Children	Children under 12 years are not allowed in front seat unless in an approved seat or harness
Traffic Lights	As in the U.S., Green means GO and Red means STOP. Amber signals to STOP until the intersection is cleared of traffic. You may then proceed safely.	
Right on Red	No	

Required Equipment	No required equipment, however, warning triangles and first aid kits are recommended
Pedestrians	Pedestrians and bicyclists have an unconditional right-of-way over vehicles turning left or right. Right-of-way in crosswalks is determined by local signage.
Tolls	There are no tolls on the Irish roadways, however, there are a few water crossings that do require a fee to ferry your car across. Prices range from €1.20 to €9.
Parking	Parking is generally free unless meters are present. The maximum time one may park at a parking meter is two hours.
Fuel	Unleaded Regular 91 octane *All are in* Unleaded Super 95 octane *English* Diesel
Motorcycles	Helmets are mandatory Headlights required at all times
Fines	Offenders have 21 days to pay their traffic fines, however parking fines may have to be paid on the spot. Be sure to get a receipt.

Drinking and Driving	You will be considered to be impaired and subject to arrest if your BAC is .08% (.8 mg.ml) or more.
U.S. State Department Traffic Safety and Road Conditions	Safety of Public Transportation: Good Urban Road Conditions/Maintenance: Good Rural Road Conditions/Maintenance: Fair Availability of Roadside Assistance: Good

EMERGENCY TELEPHONE NUMBERS

Police	999
Fire	999
Ambulance	999
US Embassy	42 Elgin Road, Ballsbridge, Dublin 4 Tel: +353 1 668-8777 Fax: +353 1 668-9946

TERMS OR WORDS YOU MAY SEE ON THE ROAD

English	Irish Gaelic
Attention	Aire
Bed and Breakfast	B&B (Leaba agus Bricfeasta)
Caution	Aireachas
Car	Gluaisteán
Car Rental Agency	Gluaisteán fostú
Detour	Timpeall
Diesel	Díosel
East	Oirthear
Entrance	Dul isteach
Exit (roadway)	Dul amach
Forbidden	Croisaim
Gasoline	Gásailín
Hospital	Ospidéal
Hotel	óstlann
Left (direction)	Clé
Motor Oil	Ola bhealaithe
Museum	Múseum
No Parking	Ná moilltear anseo
North	Tuaisceart
One-way	Sráid aontreo
Parking	Páirceaáil
Parking Lot	áit pháirceála carranna
Police	Garda
Police Station	Statiún Garda Síochana
Restaurant	Proinnteach
Right (direction)	Dheas
Road Closed	Bothár dúnta
Room for Rent	Seomera a cíos
Slow	Go mall
South	Deisceart
Street	Stráid
Truck	Trucail
Welcome	Fáilte
West	Iarthar
Yield	Tugann

(Translations courtesy of Garda Sinéad O Hara of Garda Press, and Dr Diane Cardarelli, Phd.)

18 ITALY

LOCAL SPELLING: *ITALIA*
ABBREVIATION: IT

Most travelers arrive in Italy by one of two ways. Fly into Rome, or by driving through the Alps into northern Italy. The Italian Alps provide some of the country's most spectacular scenery. Carved out by Bavarian farmers in the 8th Century, this area has relaxing spas in many of the exquisite mountain hotels and chalets. Vineyards dominate the country.

Just outside Venice, there is ample extended parking (unless your car floats) that is easy to find and navigate. Water taxis will take you through the Grand Canal to the city. Driving further south will open a world of treasures left by the Roman emperors and their armies, including medieval castles and unique Italian architecture. While all roads may lead to Rome, there are side trips to smaller towns such as Pizza, Naples and into the central mountains and on down to the southern toe. More than any other country, be sure to do your homework before traveling to Italy. There is so much history, so much to see, you will want to maximize your every moment.

While there are no public roads in the Vatican City, I could not write this book without at least mentioning it. With an area of .17 (read: point-one-seven) square miles, Vatican City is the world's smallest independent state with its own judiciary, bank, stores, postal system, seven radio stations, one television station, worldwide foreign ambassadors and an estimated population of 921. Latin is the official language, but Italian is most commonly spoken. The Euro is the official currency. You will not be allowed to enter any of the facilities without proper attire - no shorts, miniskirts or capri-style pants, no sleeveless shirts or bare shoulders.

Streets in and around the historical city centers are most often narrow and jam-packed. Italians pay little attention to the few traffic lights that exist. Rome is infamous for its traffic jams and while visiting Rome, it is highly suggested that you leave your rental car at the airport until you are ready to venture into the countryside.

Italy boasts over 5,600 miles of well maintained "Autostrada" or interstates. Italy has one of the highest rates of traffic related deaths in the European Union. High speed, alcohol or drug use contribute to the accidents occurring on the primary and secondary roads.

FAST FACTS

Area	301,230 Sq. Kilometers or 116,305 Sq. Miles slightly larger than Arizona, but long and peninsular like Florida
Primary Language	Italian, however, the northern communities in the Alps often speak the language of the neighboring countries, i.e.,German, French and Slovene.
Nationality	*noun:* Italian(s) *adjective:* Italian
Currency	Euro (EUR)
Primary Religions	Roman Catholic
Population	58,000,000
Capital / Population	Rome / 3,500,000
Other Large Cities / Population	Milan / 1,200,000 Naples / 1,000,000 Turin / 856,000 Palermo / 651,000 Genoa / 602,000

DRIVING FACTS

License	Minimum driving age is 18. A valid driver license must be accompanied with your passport.	
Speed Limits **(If not posted)**	Built up areas	50 kph / 31 mph
	Secondary Roads	90 kph / 56 mph
	Major roads outside towns	110 kph / 68 mph
	Highways	130 kph / 80 mph
Speed / Distance	Kilometers Per Hour KPH / Meters – Kilometers	
Side of the Road	Drive on the right side of the road unless One-Way	
Roundabouts	The right-of-way in the roundabout is determined by local signs. When in the roundabout, drive in a COUNTER-CLOCKWISE direction.	
Seat Belts	Front Seats	Required
	Rear Seats	Required if available
	Children	Children 3 to 12 years old must wear approved safety harness
Traffic Lights	As in the U.S., Green means GO and Red means STOP. Yellow signals to STOP until the intersection is cleared of traffic. You may then proceed safely.	
Right on Red	No, unless green arrow is present.	

Required Equipment	Warning triangle
	Safety vest (must be worn if walking to emergency phone due to breakdown)
	Spare bulb kit
	First aid kit and fire extinguisher are recommended
Pedestrians	Pedestrians and bicyclists have an unconditional right-of-way over vehicles turning left or right. Right-of-way in crosswalks is determined by local signage.
Tolls	Most of the limited access roads (Autostrade) are toll roads. You may pay with cash or with a major credit card. Like an ATM, you will have to read or hear instructions from the tollbooth credit card machine in Italian. Unlike an ATM, there will probably be a long line of impatient people behind you. Cash and a pleasant smile may get you through the tollgates most expeditiously, but plastic is always an option if short on cash.
Parking	In most of the larger cities, you must pay for street parking. Vouchers may be obtained from any of several parking kiosks and displayed on your dash or visible through the front window. Carefully check for parking instructional signs wherever you park.
Fuel	Unleaded Super 95/98 octane	*Senza Piombo*
	Diesel	*Gasolio*
Motorcycles	Helmets are mandatory
Fines	Law enforcement may collect fines during the traffic stop. Be sure to get an official receipt.

Drinking and Driving	You will be considered to be impaired and subject to arrest if your BAC is .08% (.8 mg.ml) or more.
U.S. State Department Traffic Safety and Road Conditions	Safety of Public Transportation: Good Urban Road Conditions/Maintenance: Good Rural Road Conditions/Maintenance: Good Availability of Roadside Assistance: Excellent on toll roads, Good elsewhere

EMERGENCY TELEPHONE NUMBERS

Police	113
Fire	115
Ambulance	118
US Embassy	via Vittorio Veneto 119/A 00187 Roma Tel: (+39) 06.4674.1 Fax: (+39) 06.4882.672 or 06.4674.2356

TERMS OR WORDS YOU MAY SEE ON THE ROAD

English	Italian
Attention	Attenzione
Bed and Breakfast	Bed and Breakfast
Car	Automobile
Car Rental Agency	Autonoleggio
Caution	Attenzione
Detour	Deviazione
Diesel	Diesel
East	Est
Entrance	Entrata
Exit (roadway)	Uscita
Expressway	Autostrada
Forbidden	Proibito
Gasoline	Benzina
Hospital	Ospedale
Hotel	Hotel
Left (direction)	Sinistra
Motor Oil	Lubrificante
Museum	Museo
No Parking	Divieto di Parcheggio
North	Nord
One-way	Senso Unico
Parking	Parcheggio
Parking Lot	Area di parcheggio
Passenger Vehicle	Veicolo per il trasporto passeggeri
Police	Polizia
Police Station	Satzione di Polizia
Restaurant	Ristorante
Right (direction)	Destra
Road Closed	Strada Chiusa
Room for Rent	Affittasi Stanze
Slow	Rallentare
South	Sud
Street	Strada
Toll Road	Strada a pagamento
Truck	Autotreno
Welcome	Benvenuti
West	Ovest

An excuse you might try if involved in a traffic accident. (According to urban legends, it worked in the U.S.)

Un'auto saltò fuori dal nulla, colpì la mia, e svanì.

(Translation: "An invisible car came out of nowhere, struck my vehicle, and vanished.")

A great opening line for that awkward moment you absolutely cannot think of a way to start a conversation.

La principale biblioteca dell'Università dell'Indiana sprofonda ogni anno di un pollice a causa di come è stata costruita, avendo gli ingeneri mal valutato il peso di tutti i libri ospitati nell'edificio.

(Translation: "The main Library at the Indiana University sinks over an inch every year because when it was built, engineers failed to take into account the weight of all the books that would occupy the building.")

Translation courtesy of Nicola Pedde, US Embassy, Rome

19 LIECHTENSTEIN

LOCAL SPELLING: *LIECHTENSTEIN*
ABBREVIATION: LI

While the farthest distance, border to border is just 16 miles, one might be surprised to find that there are at least two other European countries smaller in geographic area (Monaco and Vatican City). A drive through this beautiful little country will provide a pleasant break from the crowded tourist spots to which we seem to gravitate. The well maintained roads, all 155 miles of them, surrounded by the majestic Alps will take you to sleepy villages, museums, and ski lifts open summer and winter. And, best of all, you will meet warm and friendly people at every stop.

Liechtenstein has often been described as an extension of Switzerland. Regardless, it is certainly a worthy destination for a driving vacation. One ski area, Malbun, which is about ten miles (17km) from Liechtenstein's capital, Vaduz, strives very hard to accommodate off-season (warmer months) travelers. During the summer months, alpine ski areas make beautiful vistas and the drives to them are incredible. Who else do you know that can say, "This summer, we drove the roads of Liechtenstein."?

FAST FACTS

Area	160 Sq. Kilometers or 62 Sq. Miles 9/10 the size of Washington D.C.
Primary Language	German
Nationality	*noun:* Liechtensteiner(s) *adjective:* Liechtenstein
Currency	Swiss Frank (CHF)
Primary Religions	Roman Catholic 76%, Protestant 7%
Population	33,500
Capital / Population	Vaduz / 5,300
Other Large Cities / Population	Ruggell, Nendeln, Malbun, Balzers

DRIVING FACTS

License	Liechtenstein has adopted the road rules of Switzerland.
Speed Limits *(If not posted)*	Built up areas	50 kph / 31 mph
	Major roads outside towns	100 kph / 62 mph
	Highways	120 kph / 74 mph
Speed / Distance	Kilometers Per Hour KPH / Meters – Kilometers
Side of the Road	Drive on the right side of the road unless One-Way
Roundabouts	Vehicles in the roundabout have the right-of-way over vehicles entering the circle. When in the roundabout, drive in a COUNTER-CLOCKWISE direction.
Seat Belts	Front Seats	Required
	Rear Seats	Required if available
	Children	Children under 12 years old are not allowed in the front seat unless in an approved seat or harness
Traffic Lights	The rules governing traffic lights are the same as in the U.S.
Right on Red	No, unless green arrow is present.

Required Equipment	Warning triangle First aid kit Extra bulb kits and fire extinguishers are recommended.	
Pedestrians	Pedestrians and bicyclists have an unconditional right-of-way over vehicles turning left or right. Right-of-way in crosswalks is determined by local signage.	
Tolls	You must have a visible sticker allowing you to drive the Autobahn. They should come with a rental vehicle, but if you rented your car in another country, ask the rental agency if they will supply the sticker in advance. If not, you may purchase one at the National Tourist Office, Customs posts at the border, Post Offices or garages.	
Parking	Blue Zone rules apply. In most of the larger cities, you must purchase pay for street parking. Vouchers may be obtained from any of several parking kiosks and displayed on your dash or visible through the front window. Carefully check for parking instructional signs wherever you park. Tire boots are often used to secure illegally parked cars.	
Fuel	Unleaded Super 95 octane Diesel	*Bleifrei, sensa Piomba, sans Plomb* *Diesel*
Motorcycles	Helmets are mandatory Headlights required at all times	
Fines	Law enforcement may collect fines during the traffic stop. Be sure to get an official receipt.	

Drinking and Driving	You will be considered to be impaired and subject to arrest if your BAC is .08% (.8 mg.ml) or more.
U.S. State Department Traffic Safety and Road Conditions	Safety of Public Transportation: Excellent Urban Road Conditions/Maintenance: Excellent Rural Road Conditions/Maintenance: Excellent Availability of Roadside Assistance: Excellent

EMERGENCY TELEPHONE NUMBERS

Police	112
Fire	112
Ambulance	112
US Embassy	*The U.S. does not have an embassy in Liechtenstein, but the U.S. Ambassador to Switzerland is also accredited to Liechtenstein:* Jubilaumsstrasse 93 CH-3005 Bern Tel: 031-357-7011 Fax: 031-357-7344

TERMS OR WORDS YOU MAY SEE ON THE ROAD

English	German
Attention	Achtung
Bed and Breakfast	Gasthaus
Car	Auto
Car Rental Agency	Autovermietung
Caution	Vorsicht
Detour	Umleitung
Diesel	Diesel
East	Osten
Entrance	Eingang / Einfahrt
Exit (roadway)	Ausfahrt
Expressway	Autobahn
Forbidden	Verboten
Gasoline	Benzin
Hospital	Krankenhaus
Hotel	Hotel
Left (direction)	Links
Motor Oil	Motoröl
Museum	Museum
No Parking	Parken verboten
North	Norden
One-way	Einbahnstraße
Parking	Parken
Parking Lot	Parkplatz
Passenger Vehicle	Pkw, Personenwagen
Police	Polizei
Police Station	Polizeistation
Restaurant	Restaurant
Right (direction)	Rechts
Road Closed	Straße gesperrt
Room for Rent	Zimmer zu vermieten
Slow	Geschwindigkeit drosseln / Fahren sie langsamer
South	Süden
Street	Straße (strasse)
Toll Road	Mautstraße
Truck	Lkw, Lastwagen
Welcome	Wilkommen
West	Westen
Yield	Vorfahrt beachten

An excuse you might try if involved in a traffic accident. (According to urban legends, it worked in the U.S.)

Es waren ueberhaupt keine anderen Autos auf der Strasse, deswegen fuhr ich in den Bus.

(Translation: "There were absolutely no other cars on the street so I ran into the bus.")

A great opening line for that awkward moment you absolutely cannot think of a way to start a conversation.

Die meisten Staubteilchen in unserem Haus bestehen aus toter Haut.

(Translation: "Most dust particles in your house are made from dead skin.")

20 LUXEMBOURG

LOCAL SPELLING: *LUXEMBOURG*
ABBREVIATION: LU

Luxembourg, formally known as the Grand Duchy of Luxembourg, or as the locals say, Grand Duche de Luxembourg, boasts of 3,224 miles of first-class highways and roads. If you are a little confused, (Is Luxembourg a city or country?) you are not alone. Luxembourg is a country and its capitol city is Luxembourg. Things that make you want to say, "Hmmmm."

Numerous castles and fortifications are easily found throughout the countryside and stand testament to the rich past of this region. In Vianden, you can visit the most beautiful medieval castle west of the Rhine. The Luxembourg Ardennes is also a region of natural parks. There, you may visit the charming brewery-cities of Wiltz and Diekirch. Along the southeast border are vineyards alongside the Moselle River and its tributaries. These estates yield wines rated as the best in the world by many connoisseurs.

The main highways and secondary roads in Luxembourg are excellent. Roads are often narrow and winding in rural areas and very restricted in many towns. Traffic through town centers can be extremely congested, especially during rush hours. During the colder months, fog and black ice, "verglas," may make driving hazardous.

FAST FACTS

Area	2,586 Sq. Kilometers or 998 Sq. Miles half the size of Delaware
Primary Language	Luxembourgish is the national language, while German and French are also used as administrative languages
Nationality	noun: Luxembourger(s) adjective: Luxembourg
Currency	Euro (EUR)
Primary Religions	Roman Catholic 87%, Protestant 13%
Population	462,690
Capital / Population	Luxembourg / 78,800
Other Large Cities / Population	Troisviergas, Diekirch, Mertert, Grevenmacher, Diferdange, Esch, Dubelange

DRIVING FACTS

License	Minimum driving age is 18. A valid driver license must be accompanied with your passport.	
Speed Limits **(If not posted)**	Built up areas	50 kph / 31 mph
	Major roads outside towns	90 kph / 56 mph
	Highways	120 kph / 74 mph
Speed / Distance	Kilometers Per Hour KPH / Meters – Kilometers	
Side of the Road	Drive on the right side of the road unless One-Way	
Roundabouts	Vehicles in the roundabout have the right-of-way over vehicles entering the circle. When in the roundabout, drive in a COUNTER-CLOCKWISE direction.	
Seat Belts	Front Seats	Required
	Rear Seats	Required if available
	Children	Children under 12 years or under 5 feet tall are not allowed in the front seat
Traffic Lights	The rules governing traffic lights are the same as in the U.S.	
Right on Red	No	

Required Equipment	Warning triangle
	First aid kit, extra bulb kits and fire extinguishers are recommended.
Pedestrians	Pedestrians and bicyclists have an unconditional right-of-way over vehicles turning left or right. Right-of-way in crosswalks is determined by local signage.
Tolls	There are no tolls on Luxembourg's roadways.
Parking	The Blue Zone applies in the city of Luxembourg and some other cities. You may find meters or obtain receipts "discs" to place in your front windshield from a nearby kiosk. Watch for no parking signs, as cars are often booted or impounded for parking infractions.

Fuel	Unleaded Regular 95/98 octane	*Sans Plomb (FR) or Bleifrei (DE)*
	Diesel	*Gazole or Gas-oil or Gaz-oil (FR) Diesel (DE)*

Motorcycles	Helmets are mandatory
	Headlights required at all times
Fines	Law enforcement may collect fines during the traffic stop. Be sure to get an official receipt.

Drinking and Driving	You will be considered to be impaired and subject to arrest if your BAC is .08% (.8 mg.ml) or more.
U.S. State Department Traffic Safety and Road Conditions	Safety of Public Transportation: Good Urban Road Conditions/Maintenance: Good Rural Road Conditions/Maintenance: Good Availability of Roadside Assistance: Good

EMERGENCY TELEPHONE NUMBERS

Police	113
Fire	012
Ambulance	012
US Embassy	22 Boulevard Emmanuel Servais L-2535 Luxembourg Tel: +352-460123 Fax: +352-461401

TERMS OR WORDS YOU MAY SEE ON THE ROAD

> **(See Germany and France for applicable translations)**

An excuse you might try if involved in a traffic accident. (According to urban legends, it worked in the U.S.)

Le piéton ne savait pas quelle direction prendre, donc, je l'ai écrasé.

(French Translation: "The pedestrian had no idea which direction to go, so I ran over him.")

A great opening line for that awkward moment you absolutely cannot think of a way to start a conversation.

Eine Schnecke kann drei Jahre lang schlafen.

(Translation: "A snail can sleep for three years.")

21 NETHERLANDS (HOLLAND)

LOCAL SPELLING: *NEDERLAND*
ABBREVIATION: NL

First, let's help those who are confused, and those who refuse to admit they are confused about this country's name. The Netherlands is often called Holland. In reality, Holland simply encompasses the country's most populated western provinces, North (*Noord*) Holland and South (*Zuid*) Holland. The Holland provinces include such cities as Amsterdam, Rotterdam and Den Haag. To add to the confusion, their language is often called Dutch and Flemish. If you ask what the difference is, the answer may compare U.S. English and British English. The words usually sound the same but the meanings are often different. The same can be said for rural English vs. urban English, but lets not get too far off the topic.

If you fly into The Netherlands, you will probably notice expansive farm fields partitioned by elm-tree lined roads. It is believed that most of these trees were planted to shade Napoleon's armies on the march and provide wood for

their bivouacs. While these tree-lined roads are disappearing over time, in the recent past were prevalent throughout Western Europe. Typically, your tree-lined drive will be on first-rate, two-lane roads with few other cars. You may be sharing the road with bicycles, especially on the weekends. The Netherlanders are avid bicyclists and motorists must be mindful that bicycles often have the right-of-way.

Much of the country is below sea level. To control the water, the land is crisscrossed by canals that cleverly avoid interfering with their roadway system. Barges remodeled into homes are commonly seen tied to the canal walls. Many have a sign saying, "*Te Koop.*" My first (unqualified thought was that *Te Koop* translated to *tea house*, further rationalizing that it is our version of a summer cabin. Clue 1: It's a boat! Not surprisingly, the translation really means: "For Sale."

Tulips and windmills are on everyone's mind when they venture into Holland; however, the tulip season is somewhat short, March to May. Windmills, many that have been in service hundreds of years, are never out of season and can be found in almost every location of the country. Because of the low elevations, seashore roads are somewhat limited; however, the floodgates at Ooterscheidekering are quite interesting as are the surrounding beaches and coastal towns.

The Netherlands is a modern, industrialized nation, far from the dirty factory town image we so often have when the word "industrialized" is used. The country is clean, and scenery is beautiful; but, in the rural areas there are fewer hotels than commonly found throughout the rest of Europe. Start looking for accommodations around mid afternoon. If you cannot find any that suit your needs, simply drive toward a city that looks to be of some size on your map. You have my word; by sunset, you will find very satisfactory lodgings.

FAST FACTS

Area	41,526 Sq. Kilometers or 16,033 Sq. Miles About the size of ½ of South Carolina
Primary Language	Dutch[1]
Nationality	*noun:* Dutchman(men), Dutchwoman(men) *adjective:* Dutch

[1]Author's Note: Dutch and Flemish are often used synonymously. The difference between the languages has been compared to the difference between American and British English.

Currency	Euro (EUR)
Primary Religions	Roman Catholic 31%, Protestant 21%, Muslim 4%
Population	16,318,000
Capital / Population	Amsterdam (official) / 738,000
Other Large Cities / Population	The Hague (administrative capitol) / 466,000 Rotterdam / 600,000 Utrech / 264,000 Eindhoven / 207,000

DRIVING FACTS

License	Minimum driving age is 18. A valid driver license must be accompanied with your passport.	
Speed Limits **(If not posted)**	Built up areas	50 kph / 31 mph
	Major roads outside towns	100 kph / 62 mph
	Highways	120 kph / 74 mph
Speed / Distance	Kilometers Per Hour KPH / Meters – Kilometers	
Side of the Road	Drive on the right side of the road unless One-Way	
Roundabouts	The right-of-way in the roundabout is determined by local signs. When in the roundabout, drive in a COUNTER-CLOCKWISE direction.	

Seat Belts	Front Seats	Required
	Rear Seats	Required if available
	Children	• Children 0-3 years must use child safety seat
		• Children 4-11 and less than 5 feet tall in the front seat must use a child safety seat. In the back seat they may use a child safety seat belt if available.
Traffic Lights	As in the U.S., <u>Green</u> means GO and <u>Red</u> means STOP. <u>Orange</u> signals to STOP until the intersection is cleared of traffic. You may then proceed safely.	
Right on Red	No, unless green arrow is present.	
Required Equipment	Neither warning triangle, first aid kit, extra bulb kits nor fire extinguishers are required, but all are recommended.	
Pedestrians	Pedestrians and bicyclists have an unconditional right-of-way over vehicles turning left or right. Right-of-way in crosswalks is determined by local signage.	
Tolls	You may find small tolls charged at some bridges and tunnels. There are no tolls on the roadways.	
Parking	The Blue Zone system applies in most of the larger cities. You may find meters or obtain receipts "discs" to place in your front windshield from police stations or a nearby kiosk. Carefully check for parking instructional signs wherever you park.	
Fuel	Unleaded Regular 95/98 octane	*Loodvrije benzine*
	Diesel	*Diesel*

Motorcycles	Helmets are mandatory
Fines	Law enforcement may collect fines during the traffic stop. Be sure to get an official receipt.
Drinking and Driving	You will be considered to be impaired and subject to arrest if your BAC is .05% (.5 mg.ml) or more.
Misc.	The use of cellular telephones while driving is illegal without the use of a "hands-free" device. Lanes at the center of many urban two-way streets are reserved for buses, trams and taxis. Pedestrians should not walk along bicycle paths, which are often on the sidewalk and usually designated by red pavement.
U.S. State Department Traffic Safety and Road Conditions	Safety of Public Transportation: Excellent Urban Road Conditions/Maintenance: Excellent Rural Road Conditions/Maintenance: Excellent Availability of Roadside Assistance: Excellent

EMERGENCY TELEPHONE NUMBERS

Police	112
Fire	112
Ambulance	112
US Embassy	Lange Voorhout 102 2514 EJ The Hague Tel: +31 70 310-9209 Fax: +31 70 361-4688

TERMS OR WORDS YOU MAY SEE ON THE ROAD

English	Dutch
Attention	*Let op!*
Bed and Breakfast	*Logies en ontbijt*
Car	*Auto*
Car Rental Agency	*Autoverhuurbedrijf*
Caution	*Voorzichtig*
Detour	*Wegomleiding*
Diesel	*Diesel*
East	*Oost*
Entrance	*Oprit*
Exit (building)	*Uitrit*
Exit (roadway)	*Afrit*
Expressway	*Snelweg*
Forbidden	*Verboden*
Gasoline	*Benzine*
Hospital	*Ziekenhuis*
Hotel	*Hotel*
Left (direction)	*Links*
Motor Oil	*Motorolie*
Museum	*Museum*
No Parking	*Verboden te Parkeren*
North	*Noord*
One-way	*Eenrichtingverkeer*
Parking	*Parkeren*
Parking Lot	*Parkeerplaats*
Police	*Politie*
Police Station	*Politiebureau*
Restaurant	*Restaurant*
Right (direction)	*Rechts*
Road Closed	*Weg afgesloten/geen doorgang*
Room for Rent	*Kamer te huur*
Slow Down	*Langzaam Rijden*
South	*Zuid*
Street	*Straat*
Toll Road	*Tolweg*
Truck	*Vrachtwagen*
Welcome	*Welkom*
West	*West*
Yield	*Voorrang verlenen*

An excuse you might try if involved in a traffic accident. (According to urban legends, it worked in the U.S.)

Ik zag hoe de triest uitziende oude man door de auto geschept werd en via de motorkap in de lucht werd gelanceerd.

(Translation: "I saw the slow-moving, sad-faced old gentleman as he bounced off the hood of my car.")

A great opening line for that awkward moment you absolutely cannot think of a way to start a conversation.

De sigaret was eerder uitgevonden dan de lucifer.

(Translation: "The cigarette was invented before the match.")

22 NORWAY

LOCAL SPELLING: *NORGE*
ABBREVIATION: NO

Europe's most northern country is Norway. Norway's mountains plunging into its jagged seacoast create a breathtaking landscape. If my theory about the journey, not the destination, is important, you will thrive in Norway. Some may have to adjust to the lower speed limits that reflect the Norwegian way of life, delightfully relaxed. You will find windy, well-maintained roads often passing through long tunnels. The scenery is spectacular and you have an excellent chance of seeing the ever-present moose, sheep and reindeer in their natural habitat. Watch carefully; a moose-and-car-fender-story will not strike the funny bone of most rental agents. It is strongly suggested that driving vacations be taken during the summer months as the winter conditions may be extreme.

During the summer months, those who venture into the Arctic Circle will have an opportunity to view the Land of the Midnight Sun from the middle of May to the end of July. Folks who brave the Norwegian winter are treated to a spectacular display of the aurora borealis, otherwise known as the Northern Lights, the flaming spectacle of the Arctic winter sky. The National Oceanographic and Atmospheric

Administration's (NOAA) Space Environment Center web page (**http://www.sec.noaa.gov/index.html**) is an excellent resource for determining the best times to view the Northern Lights.

Although this book is about driving vacations, Norway's beauty is always measured by its fjords. Day trips and overnighters to and through the fjords may be found with ease. One should not come to Norway without experiencing some of the magic of its coastline. Most of the best driving locations are in the southern portion of the country. For the adventurous, a single highway treks to Norway's northern most boundaries. Gas up every chance you get and bring some snacks. If unique driving experiences on high scenic roads intrigue you, you will not be disappointed in the northern drive.

FAST FACTS

Area	324,220 Sq. Kilometers or 125,182 Sq. Miles Slightly larger than New Mexico
Primary Language	Bokmal Norwegian, Nynorsk Norwegian
Nationality	*noun:* Norwegian(s) *adjective:* Noregian
Currency	Euro (EUR)
Primary Religions	Evangelical Lutheran 86%, other Protestant, Roman Catholic
Population	4,600,000
Capital / Population	Oslo / 790,000
Other Large Cities / Population	Bergen / 211,000 Stavanger / 168,000 Trondheim / 144,000

DRIVING FACTS

License	Minimum driving age is 18. A valid driver license must be accompanied with your passport.	
Speed Limits **(If not posted)**	Built up areas	50 kph / 31 mph
	Major roads outside towns	80 kph / 50 mph
	Highways	90 kph / 56 mph
Speed / Distance	Kilometers Per Hour KPH / Meters – Kilometers	
Side of the Road	Drive on the right side of the road unless One-Way	
Roundabouts	Vehicles in the roundabout have the right-of-way over vehicles entering the circle. When in the roundabout, drive in a COUNTER-CLOCKWISE direction.	
Seat Belts	Front Seats	Required
	Rear Seats	Required if available
	Children	Children under 4 years of age must use an approved seat restraint.
Traffic Lights	The rules governing traffic lights are the same as in the U.S.	
Right on Red	No, unless green arrow is present.	

Required Equipment	Warning triangle.
Pedestrians	Pedestrians and bicyclists have an unconditional right-of-way over vehicles turning left or right. Right-of-way in crosswalks is determined by local signage.
Tolls	Several roads have tolls, so be sure to have ample pocket change. There are also tolls assessed for vehicles entering the town centers of some of the larger cities. Cash only; credit cards are not accepted at toll booths.
Parking	Parking on main roads or on bends is not allowed. A sign that reads "All stans forbudt" means No Stopping Allowed. Parking meters are differentiated as follows: Yellow = one-hour, Grey = two-hour, Brown = three-hour. Parking regulations are strictly enforced.

Fuel	Unleaded Regular 95/98 octane	*Loodvrije benzine*
	Diesel	*Diesel*

Motorcycles	Helmets are mandatory. Headlights required at all times.
Fines	Law enforcement may collect fines during the traffic stop. Be sure to get an official receipt.

Drinking and Driving	You will be considered to be impaired and subject to arrest if your BAC is .02% (.2 mg.ml) or more.
Misc.	Headlights must be on at all times while driving. Automatic cameras are placed on roadways by police to help maintain speed limits, which are generally slower than other European countries.
U.S. State Department Traffic Safety and Road Conditions	Safety of Public Transportation: Good Urban Road Conditions/Maintenance: Good Rural Road Conditions/Maintenance: Fair Availability of Roadside Assistance: Fair

EMERGENCY TELEPHONE NUMBERS

Police	112
Fire	110
Ambulance	113
US Embassy	Drammensveien 18, 0244 Oslo Tel: (47) 22448550

TERMS OR WORDS YOU MAY SEE ON THE ROAD

English	Norwegian
Bed and Breakfast	(all hotels are bed and breakfasts)
Car	Bil
Car Rental Agency	Bilutleiefirma or more used Bilutleie
Caution	Forsiktig
Danger	Fare
Detour	Omkjøring
Diesel	Diesel
East	Øst
Entrance	Innkjørsel or Inn (In)
Exit (roadway)	Utkjørsel or Ut (Out)
Expressway	Motorvei
Forbidden	Forbudt
Gasoline	Bensin
Hospital	Sykehus
Hotel	Hotel
Left (direction)	Venstre
Motor Oil	Motorolje
Museum	Museum
No Parking	Ingen parkering or Parkering forbudt
No Stopping	All stans forbudt or NB
North	Nord
One-way	Enveiskjørt or Påbudt kjøreretning
Parking	Parkering
Parking Lot	Parkeringsplass
Passenger Vehicle	Personbil
Police	Politi
Restaurant	Restaurant
Right (direction)	Høyre
Road Closed	Veien er stengt
Road Work	Veiarbeide
Rock or Snow Slide	Ras
Room for Rent	Rom til leie
Slow	Sakte
South	Sør or Syd
Street	Gate
Toll Road	Toll road - (cash only - no credit cards)
Truck	Lastebil
Welcome	Velkommen
West	Vest
Yield	Vike
Yield right of way	Vikeplikt

My favorite Norwegian roadway sign is: *Stor Elgfare*

Which translates to: *EXTREME DANGER - MOOSE ON ROAD*

Not to be taken lightly, this sign must be taken seriously.

23 POLAND

LOCAL SPELLING: *POLSKA*
ABBREVIATION: PL

1989 marked the beginning of a new, United Europe. The Iron Curtain was torn down, opening the former Soviet block countries to free travel. Poland quickly became one of the countries most frequently visited. While the country initially had its problems with organized crime, aggressive efforts were taken to gain control of their country. Polish government literature states: "...statistics consistently show Poland to be at least as safe as the rest of Europe or even safer than some Western countries."

Poles often describe their country as, "a garden of nature." Famous for its lakes and rivers, Poland features 23 national parks that represent the variety of its landscapes and ecosystems. Eco-tourism is a budding enterprise throughout the country. Numerous historical buildings, country manors and castles operate as hotels and are usually situated in areas attractive for tourists. The best bang for your buck may be found by tracing the edge of the Baltic Sea in the northwest corner of the country and down along the German-Poland border. You will be away from the city noise, often in the middle of well-established national parks, and have ample opportunities to experience Poland's excellent and unique cuisine. (Be sure to sample a cup or bowl of *borscht* during your travels. Hot or cold, it very well may be the best soup you have ever enjoyed.) Drive deeper into the country to discover many of the cultural riches of Poland's past and present. With scores of museums, theatres and shopping centers, Warsaw is a prime tourist attraction. Common to many larger European cities, Warsaw's traffic is near capacity and a true headache to navigate. The area surrounding Warsaw, however, offers many opportunities on less traveled roads. Visitors are often drawn to the small village of Zelazowa Wola, the birthplace and childhood home of composer Fryderyk Chopin. It is to be found among the picturesque meadows 30 miles west of Warsaw on the Utrata

River. The park surrounding the Chopin Manor house is considered one of the most beautiful properties in Poland.

If traveling into Poland from other countries, carefully read your car rental contract to avoid legal problems while crossing the border. Many auto rental companies prohibit their vehicles from entering Poland. Expect the roads to be a little rougher and slower than you may be accustomed to. This aside, Poland is certainly worth consideration when searching for new territories to explore.

FAST FACTS

Area	312,685 Sq. Kilometers or 120,728 Sq. Miles Slightly smaller than New Mexico
Primary Language	Polish
Nationality	*noun:* Pole(s) *adjective:* Polish
Currency	Zloty (PLN)
Primary Religions	Roman Catholic 95%, Eastern Orthodox, Protestant
Population	38,500,000
Capital / Population	Warsaw / 2,202,000
Other Large Cities / Population	Lodz / 778,000 Krakow / 733,000 Wroclaw 632,000 Poznan / 581,000 Gdansk / 457,000 Szczecin / 416,000

DRIVING FACTS

License	Minimum driving age is 17. On July 1, 1999, new regulations governing the issuance and use of driver licenses entered into force. In order to drive in Poland, American citizens must have either an International Driving Permit or a Polish national driver license: a U.S. State driving license without an IDP is insufficient.
Speed Limits **(If not posted)**	Built up areas — 50 kph / 31 mph; Major roads outside towns — 100 kph / 62 mph; Highways — 130 kph / 80 mph
Speed / Distance	Kilometers Per Hour KPH / Meters – Kilometers
Side of the Road	Drive on the right side of the road unless One-Way
Roundabouts	Vehicles in the roundabout have the right-of-way over vehicles entering the circle. When in the roundabout, drive in a COUNTER-CLOCKWISE direction.
Seat Belts	Front Seats — Required; Rear Seats — Required if available; Children — Children under 10 years of age are not allowed in the front seat unless in an approved child restraint seat or harness.
Traffic Lights	The rules governing traffic lights are the same as in the U.S.
Right on Red	No, unless green arrow is present.

Required Equipment	Warning triangle Fire extinguishers Extra bulb kits and are recommended.
Pedestrians	Pedestrians and bicyclists have an unconditional right-of-way over vehicles turning left or right. Right-of-way in crosswalks is determined by local signage.
Tolls	There are no tolls on Poland's roadways.
Parking	The Blue Zone system applies in most of the larger cities. You may find meters or obtain receipts "discs" to place in your front windshield from police stations or a nearby kiosk. To keep from having to carry small change for parking machines, you may wish to buy a parking card, which may be used in all machines. Carefully check for parking instructional signs wherever you park.

Fuel	Unleaded Regular 91 octane	*Benzyna bezolowiu*
	Diesel	*Diesel*

Motorcycles	Helmets are mandatory Headlights required at all times
Fines	Law enforcement may collect fines during the traffic stop. Be sure to get an official receipt.

Drinking and Driving	You will be considered to be impaired and subject to arrest if your BAC is .02% (.2 mg.ml) or more.
Misc.	• Between October 1 and April 1, you are required to have your headlights on at all times. For the rest of the year, turn them on between dusk and dawn. • The use of cellular phones while driving is prohibited, except for "hands-free" models.
U.S. State Department Traffic Safety and Road Conditions	Safety of Public Transportation: Fair Urban Road Conditions/Maintenance: Fair Rural Road Conditions/Maintenance: Poor Availability of Roadside Assistance: Fair

EMERGENCY TELEPHONE NUMBERS

Police	997
Fire	998
Ambulance	999
US Embassy	Al. Ujazdowskie 29/31 00-540 Warsaw Tel.: +48/22 504-2000 Fax: +48/22 504-2688

TERMS OR WORDS YOU MAY SEE ON THE ROAD

English	Polish
Attention	*Uwaga*
Bed and Breakfast	*Kwatery prywante (B&B)*
Car	*Samochod*
Car Rental Agency	*Agencja Wynajmu Samochodow*
Caution	*Ostroznie*
Detour	*Objazd*
Diesel	*Olej Napediwy*
East	*Wschod*
Entrance	*Entrance*
Exit (building)	*Wyjście*
Exit (roadway)	*Zjazd*
Expressway	*Autostrada*
Forbidden	*Zabronione*
Gasoline	*Stacja Benzynowa*
Hospital	*Szpital*
Hotel	*Hotel*
Left (direction)	*Na lewo*
Motor Oil	*Olej Silnikowy*
Museum	*Muzeum*
No Parking	*Nie parkowac*
North	*Polnoc*
One-way	*Jednokierunkowa*
Parking	*Parking*
Parking Lot	*Parking Lot*
Passenger Vehicle	*Samochod pasazerski*
Police	*Policja*
Police Station	*Posterunke Policji*
Restaurant	*Restauracja*
Right (direction)	*Na prawo*
Road Closed	*Droga zamknieta*
Room for Rent	*Pokoj do wynajecia*
Slow	*Wolniej*
South	*Poludnie*
Street	*Ulica*
Toll Road	*Droga Glowna*
Truck	*Samochod ciezarowy*
Welcome	*Zapraszamy*
West	*Zachod*

An excuse you might try if involved in a traffic accident. (According to urban legends, it worked in the U.S.)

Facei zajmowak caka drogę, dlatego husiacem ostro skręcać, aby go stuknoć.

(Translation: "The guy was all over the road, I had to swerve a number of times to hit him.")

A great opening line for that awkward moment you absolutely cannot think of a way to start a conversation.

Jest fizycznie niemozliwe, aby polizać swój kokied.

(Translation: "It is physically impossible to lick your elbow.")

Translation courtesy of Grzegorz Gryz, Police Insignia Collector

24 PORTUGAL

LOCAL SPELLING: *PORTUGAL*
ABBREVIATION: PT

With territories and colonies around the globe, Portugal was once a world power in its own right. Although the country relinquished its overseas holdings, it has maintained the culture and charm from years past.

Seemingly two worlds apart, but only a few hours drive separate the beautiful and contrasting regions of Minho and Alentejo. Minho, in the most northwestern corner of Portugal offers the September grape harvest which presents an opportunity to sample the region's famous food, drink, and enthusiastic hospitality. You will share the road with grape-laden oxcarts as vineyards famous for their *vinho verde* are harvested by hand.

Traveling south takes you across the Tagus River valley, a treasure in its own right. You may discover each township's unique personality as you drive south along the Spanish border or trace the coastline for exhilarating ocean-road cruising. The second most southerly region is Alentejo. You will believe you are in a different world! Expansive plains safeguarded by medieval castles replace vineyards and valleys of Minho. Sturdy cork and aged olive trees grace an endless cobalt sky. The Alentejo Region is a delight for its visitors with its palaces, churches, museums, archaeological sites and fine sandy beaches. Picturesque whitewashed villages are nestled in their hilltop perches unchanged by the centuries. Algarve is Portugal's southernmost province and has a coastline rich with golden sandy beaches in spectacular settings.

While the main highways have been significantly upgraded in recent years, use special caution when venturing off the *via rápida* (expressway). Portugal has one of the highest rates of automobile accidents and traffic related fatalities in Europe. Drivers should use extreme caution, as local driving habits, high speeds, and poorly marked roads pose special hazards. Fines for traffic violations are substantial and usually must be paid on the spot.

A word of caution: If you are caught using a cell phone while driving, it may cost you a 200€ (Euros) fine.

FAST FACTS

Area	92,391 Sq. Kilometers or 35,672 Sq. Miles Slightly smaller than Indiana
Primary Language	Portuguese
Nationality	*noun:* Portuguese (singular and plural) *adjective:* Portuguese
Currency	Euro (EUR)
Primary Religions	Roman Catholic 94%, Protestant
Population	10,500,000
Capital / Population	Lisbon / 2,600,000
Other Large Cities / Population	Oporto / 264,000

DRIVING FACTS

License	Minimum driving age is 17. Visitors may drive on a U.S. Driver's License for up to 6 months.	
Speed Limits **(If not posted)**	Built up areas	50 kph / 31 mph
	Major roads outside towns	90-100 kph / 56-62 mph
	Highways	120 kph / 74 mph
Speed / Distance	Kilometers Per Hour KPH / Meters – Kilometers	
Side of the Road	Drive on the right side of the road unless One-Way	
Roundabouts	Vehicles in the roundabout have the right-of-way over vehicles entering the circle. When in the roundabout, drive in a COUNTER-CLOCKWISE direction.	
Seat Belts	Front Seats	Required
	Rear Seats	Required if available
	Children	• Children under 12 years old are not allowed in a front seat unless in an approved child restraint. • Babies under 3 years of age must be in an approved infant seat
Traffic Lights	As in the U.S., Green means GO and Red means STOP. Yellow signals to STOP until the intersection is cleared of traffic. You may then proceed safely.	
Right on Red	No, unless green arrow is present.	

Required Equipment	Warning triangle Extra bulb kits and fire extinguishers are recommended.	
Pedestrians	Portugal is the exception to most of the rest of the civilized world; pedestrians and cyclists never have the right-of-way unless indicated by traffic signals or signs.	
Tolls	There are tolls on several of the expressways, and must be paid in cash; fees vary.	
Parking	The Blue Zone system applies in some of the larger cities, and you may also find parking meters. You may obtain receipts "discs" to place in your front windshield from police stations or a nearby kiosk. Carefully check for parking instructional signs wherever you park. Parking within 18 meters of a road junction, 15 meters of a bus stop or within 3 meters of a tram or bus stop, is prohibited.	
Fuel	Unleaded Super 95/98 octane Diesel	*Sem Chumbo* or *Gasolina sin Plomo* *Gasoleo*
Motorcycles	Helmets are mandatory Headlights required at all times	
Fines	Law enforcement may collect fines during the traffic stop. Be sure to get an official receipt.	

Drinking and Driving	You will be considered to be impaired and subject to arrest if your BAC is .05% (.5 mg.ml) or more.
U.S. State Department Traffic Safety and Road Conditions	Safety of Public Transportation: Good Urban Road Conditions/Maintenance: Fair Rural Road Conditions/Maintenance: Poor Availability of Roadside Assistance: Fair

EMERGENCY TELEPHONE NUMBERS

Police	112
Fire	112
Ambulance	112
US Embassy	Avenida das Forças Armadas 1600-081 LISBON Tel: 21-7273127 Fax: 21-7266219

TERMS OR WORDS YOU MAY SEE ON THE ROAD

English	Portugese
Attention	Atenção
Bed and Breakfast	Dormida e Pequeno-almoço
Car	Carro
Car Rental Agency	Aluguer de automóveis
Caution	Cautela
Detour	Desvio
Diesel	Diesel
East	Este
Entrance	Entrada
Exit (building)	Saída
Exit (roadway)	Saída
Expressway	Via rápida
Forbidden	Proíbido
Gasoline	Gasolina
Hospital	Hospital
Left (direction)	Esquerda
Motor Oil	Óleo do motor
Museum	Museu
No Parking	Estacionamento proíbido
North	Norte
One-way	Sentido único
Parking	Estacionamento
Parking Lot	Parque de estacionamento
Passenger Vehicle	Passageiro
Police	Polícia
Police Station	Esquadra de polícia
Restaurant	Restaurante
Right (direction)	Direita
Road Closed	Estrada fechada
Room for Rent	Quarto para alugar
Slow	Devagar
South	Sul
Street	Estrada
Toll Road	Portagem
Truck	Veículo pesado
Welcome	Bemvindo
West	Oeste
Yield	Dar prioridade

An excuse you might try if involved in a traffic accident. (According to urban legends, it worked in the U.S.)

Eu fui contra o camião porque o meu patrão ligou-me pelo telemovel.

(Translation: "I ran into the truck because my boss called me on the telephone.")

A great opening line for that awkward moment you absolutely cannot think of a way to start a conversation.

Apenas uma em dois mil milhões de pessoas vive até aos 116 anos ou mais.

(Translation: "Only one person in two billion will live to be 116 or older.")

Translation courtesy of Manuel Pereira of the Portuguese Embassy and Comissário Hugo Palma, Portuguese Police

25 SPAIN

LOCAL SPELLING: *ESPANA*
ABBREVIATION: ES

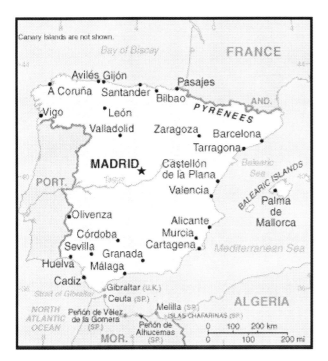

If you believe bullfights and sangria typify Spain, you are in for a splendid surprise. Spain is a country of contradiction, and deceptively diverse. From Pyrenees Mountains through her central plains, to the Gold Coast on the Mediterranean Sea, one can travel windy roads to abandoned castles, scenic villages and beautiful, panoramic views.

In the extreme northwest is a region called Galicia, which is known in Spain as the "land of the 1,000 rivers." There you can explore the ancient pilgrimage route known as the *Camino de Santiago*. The Mediterranean coast offers stimulating roads bordering high cliffs and white beaches. Be sure not to miss Alicante, once touted as the chocolate capitol of the world.

Many of the rural roads are very narrow. You might even consider pulling your mirrors in as you pass through some of the smaller villages. When driving during the night in rural areas, the roads will be poorly lit. Be watchful for farm animals and poorly marked roads. Rural traffic is generally heavier in July and August as well as during the Christmas and Easter holidays.

FAST FACTS

Area	504,782 Sq. Kilometers or 194,897 Sq. Miles A little larger than California
Primary Language	Castilian Spanish
Nationality	*noun:* Spaniard(s) *adjective:* Spanish
Currency	Euro (EUR)
Primary Religions	Roman Catholic 94%
Population	40,281,000
Capital / Population	Madrid / 5,130,000
Other Large Cities / Population	Barcelona / 1,529,000 Valencia / 741,000

DRIVING FACTS

License	A valid driver license must be accompanied with your passport.
Speed Limits *(If not posted)*	Built up areas · 50 kph / 31 mph Major roads outside towns · 100 kph / 62 mph Highways · 120 kph / 74 mph
Speed / Distance	Kilometers Per Hour KPH / Meters – Kilometers
Side of the Road	Drive on the right side of the road unless One-Way
Roundabouts	Vehicles in the roundabout have the right-of-way over vehicles entering the circle. When in the roundabout, drive in a COUNTER-CLOCKWISE direction.
Seat Belts	Front Seats · Required Rear Seats · Required if available Children · • Under 12 years and less than 1.5 meters are not allowed in front seat unless in an approved seat or harness
Traffic Lights	As in the U.S., Green means GO and Red means STOP. Yellow signals to STOP until the intersection is cleared of traffic. You may then proceed safely.
Right on Red	No, unless green arrow is present.

Required Equipment	2 Warning triangles Spare bulb kit Spare wheel Reflective safety vest	
Pedestrians	Pedestrians and bicyclists have an unconditional right-of-way over vehicles turning left or right. Right-of-way in crosswalks is determined by local signage.	
Tolls	There are tolls on several of the expressways and tunnels.	
Parking	Blue painted curbs often allow parking for residents only; check for signs. The Blue Zone system applies in most of the larger cities. You may find meters or obtain receipts "discs" to place in your front windshield from hotels, travel agencies and city centers. The safest place to park is in a garage, but check for prices before you enter to avoid a pricey surprise. Parking is sometimes determined by the day of the month. Parking is allowed on the even numbered side on even days and on the odd numbered side on the odd days. Illegally parked vehicles may be towed, so watch for signs.	
Fuel	Unleaded Super 95 octane Diesel	*Gasolina sin plomo* *Gasoleo*
Motorcycles	Helmets are mandatory on motorcycles over 125cc Headlights required at all times	
Fines	Law enforcement may collect fines during the traffic stop. Be sure to get an official receipt.	

Drinking and Driving	You will be considered impaired and subject to arrest if your BAC is .05% (.5 mg.ml) or more.
Misc.	The use of a mobile phone without a hands-free device while driving a car is prohibited. There is a fine of 150 euros for violation of this regulation and loss of driving privileges.
U.S. State Department Traffic Safety and Road Conditions	Safety of Public Transportation: Good Urban Road Conditions/Maintenance: Excellent Rural Road Conditions/Maintenance: Good Availability of Roadside Assistance: Good

EMERGENCY TELEPHONE NUMBERS

Police	091
Fire	080
Ambulance	092
US Embassy	Calle Serrano 75 28006 Madrid Tel: (34) 91 587 2240 Fax: (34) 91 587 2243

TERMS OR WORDS YOU MAY SEE ON THE ROAD

English	Castilian Spanish
Attention	Atencion
Bed and Breakfast	Cama y Desayuno
Car	Coche
Dander	Peligro
Detour	Una Desviacion
Diesel	Diesel
East	Este
Entrance	Entrada
Exit (building)	Salida
Exit (roadway)	Salida de Carretera
Forbidden	Prohibido
Gasoline	Gasolina
Expressway	Autopista
Hospital	Hospital
Hotel	Hotel
Left(direction)	Izquierda
Motor Oil	Aceite de Motor
Museum	Museo
No Parking	No aparcamiento
North	Norte
One-way	De Direccion Unica
Parking	Aparcamiento
Parking Lot	Espacio de Aparcar
Passenger Vehicle	Vehiculo de Pasageros
Police	Policia
Police Station	Estacion de Policia
Restaurant	Restaurante
Right (direction)	Derecha
Road Closed	Carratera Cerrada
Room for Rent	Habitacion Para Alquilar
Slow	Despacio
South	Sur
Street	Calle
Toll Road	Peaje
Truck	Camion
Welcome	Bienvendo
West	Oeste
Yield	Ceda el Paso

An excuse you might try if involved in a traffic accident. (According to urban legends, it worked in the U.S.)

Cuando me acerqué al cruce de trafico aparecio una señal que anteriormente no estaba allí. No pude para a tiempo para evitar el acidente.

(Translation: "As I approached the intersection a sign suddenly appeared in a place where no stop sign had ever appeared before. I was unable to stop in time to avoid the accident.")

A great opening line for that awkward moment you absolutely cannot think of a way to start a conversation.

Las mariposas saborean con sus patas...

(Translation: "Butterflies taste with their feet.")

Translation courtesy of Chela Decker and David Powers

26 SWEDEN

LOCAL SPELLING: *SVERIGE*
ABBREVIATION: SE

The population of Sweden is less than that of Holland and Belgium; however, Sweden is one of Europe's largest countries. While Swedish is the official language, almost every citizen speaks English fluently. The large area and sparse population are a perfect fit for abundant fresh air, clean water, pristine forests, unspoiled beaches and vast areas of wilderness. Sweden offers drivers a well-maintained network of roads and highways. Traffic jams are rare and one will find easy to understand road signs.

One of the most enjoyable and scenic drives of Sweden is between Stockholm through the town of Mora and around Lake Silja. The picturesque landscape around Siljan was shaped 360 million years ago by one of the world's largest meteorite impacts. On the crater slopes in the winter, skiing and snowboarding are popular activities. This is one of Sweden's number one tourist destinations for the locals. During the first week of July every year, one of Sweden's leading music festivals, "Musik vid Siljan," is held. The festival includes folk music, jazz and popular music. "Leksand, Tällberg, Rättvik and Mora are some of the sites for "Musik vid Siljan."

Beware; you must use your headlights 24 hours a day. Vast mountains in the northern area called Lapland, deep pine forests in Central Sweden and clear blue lakes and rivers that flow from the snow-capped mountains in the west into the Baltic in the east. All this, framed by a beautiful coastline, make Sweden an excellent choice for a driving vacation.

FAST FACTS

Area	449,964 Sq. Kilometers or 173,732 Sq. Miles Slightly larger than California
Primary Language	Swedish
Nationality	*noun:* Swede(s) *adjective:* Swedish
Currency	Swedish krona (SEK)
Primary Religions	Lutheran 87%
Population	9,000,000
Capital / Population	Stockholm / 1,622,000
Other Large Cities / Population	Göteborg / 507,000 Malmö / 245,000

DRIVING FACTS

License	Minimum driving age is 18. A valid driver license must be accompanied with your passport.
Speed Limits *(If not posted)*	Built up areas 50 kph / 31 mph Major roads outside towns 90 kph / 56 mph Highways 110 kph / 68 mph
Speed / Distance	Kilometers Per Hour KPH / Meters – Kilometers
Side of the Road	Drive on the right side of the road unless One-Way
Roundabouts	Vehicles in the roundabout have the right-of-way over vehicles entering the circle. When in the roundabout, drive in a COUNTER-CLOCKWISE direction.
Seat Belts	Front Seats Required Rear Seats Required if available Children • Under 7 years should be use an approved child restraint or harness.
Traffic Lights	As in the U.S., <u>Green</u> means GO and <u>Red</u> means STOP. <u>Yellow</u> signals to STOP until the intersection is cleared of traffic. You may then proceed safely. <u>Red+Yellow</u> signal means PREPARE TO GO.
Right on Red	No, unless green arrow is present.

Required Equipment	Warning triangle First aid kit and fire extinguishers are recommended.
Pedestrians	Pedestrians and bicyclists have an unconditional right-of-way over vehicles turning left or right. Right-of-way in crosswalks is determined by local signage.
Tolls	There are no tolls except when crossing the Øresund Bridge.
Parking	Parking violations may result in very expensive fines in Sweden. Most Swedish cities operate on both metered on-street parking and timed ticket machines from 8 a.m. to 6 p.m. Only park on the right side of the road. A yellow sign with a red line across the bottom means parking is restricted in the area. When in doubt, ask.
Fuel	Unleaded Regular 95 octane *Blyfri 95* Unleaded Super 98 octane *Blyfri 98* Diesel *Diesel*
Motorcycles	Helmets are mandatory Headlights required at all times
Fines	Law enforcement may collect fines during the traffic stop. Be sure to get an official receipt.

Drinking and Driving	You will be considered to be impaired and subject to arrest if your BAC is .02% (.2 mg.ml) or more.
U.S. State Department Traffic Safety and Road Conditions	Safety of Public Transportation: Good Urban Road Conditions/Maintenance: Good Rural Road Conditions/Maintenance: Good Availability of Roadside Assistance: Good

EMERGENCY TELEPHONE NUMBERS

Police	112
Fire	112
Ambulance	112
US Embassy	Dag Hammarskjölds Väg 31 SE-115 89 Stockholm Tel: (+46) 8 783 5300

TERMS OR WORDS YOU MAY SEE ON THE ROAD

English	Swedish
Attention	Se upp!
Bed and Breakfast	Bed & Breakfast
Car	Bil
Car Rental Agency	Biluthyrningsfirma
Caution	Varning
Detour	Omväg
Diesel	Diesel
East	Öster
Entrance	Infart
Exit (roadway)	Avfart
Expressway	Motorväg
Forbidden	Förbjuden
Gasoline	Bensin
Hospital	Lasarett
Hotel	Hotell
Left (direction)	Vänster
Motor Oil	Motorolja
Museum	Museum
No Parking	Förbud att parkera fordon
North	Norr
One-way	Enkelriktad
Parking	Parkering
Parking Lot	Parkeringsplats
Passenger Vehicle	Personbil
Police	Polis
Police Station	Polis Station
Restaurant	Restaurang
Right (direction)	Höger
Road Closed	Vagen avstängd (Vägen avstängd)
Room for Rent	Rum att hyra
Slow	Sakta
South	Söder
Street	Gata
Toll Road	Avgiftsbelagd väg
Truck	Lastbil
Welcome	Vlkommen
West	Väster
Yield	Väjningsplikt

An excuse you might try if involved in a traffic accident. (According to urban legends, it worked in the U.S.)

Fotgängare här tanke inte vilka riktning till springa, så jag springa kom sig!

(Translation: "The pedestrian had no idea which direction to run, so I ran over him.")

A great opening line for that awkward moment you absolutely cannot think of a way to start a conversation.

Jag blir nervös när jag ska tala svenska.

(Translation: "I get nervous when I speak Swedish.")

Translations courtesy of Ulf T. Häggman and James Epperson.

27 SWITZERLAND

LOCAL SPELLING: *SCHWEIZ (GERMAN)*
SUISSE (FRENCH) SVIZZERA (ITALIAN)
ABBREVIATION: CH

Typically, when one thinks of the Alps, they envision Switzerland. The country is an extraordinary mixture of high mountain glaciers with dramatic peaks occupying more than half of the country coupled with a mix of forests, meadows, pastures and peaceful lakes. The roads traversing Switzerland are excellent and lead between villages, towns and farm houses that defy the most picturesque tourist posters. You may take your camera, but you will never catch the majesty of the Alpine mountains. There is no possible way one could fully enjoy the Alpine experience riding in a tour bus. Interlaken (translation: Between the Lakes) is

one of the more popular destinations. It is a little southwest of the center of the country, and during the winter a premier ski destination. From Interlaken, you will have quick access by train to the Jungfraujoch research station which is 11,782 feet above sea level. There you can walk in tunnels bored through glaciers and stand on the edge of cliffs more than a mile high. On the way up, you will also see the Eiger, made popular by the movie "The Eiger Sanction."

Head south to the border and you will find the town of Zermat at the base of the Matterhorn, one of Europes most popular mountains for professional climbers. Zermat, like Venice, is not accessible by car. Long-term parking is easily found below Zermat and a train will take you to town and out of the rigors of city life as we know it. Zermat is a truly unique experience.

Should you drive Switzerland's northern borders, you will surely find many pleasing villages along the Rhine. July and August offer acres upon acres of beautiful sunflowers, one of Switzerland's many commercial crops. Regardless of the time of year, when you traverse the Alps, prepare yourself for freezing temperatures as you pass through the highest points.

FAST FACTS

Area	15,942 Sq. Kilometers or 6,155 Sq. Miles A little larger than Maryland
Primary Language	German (64%) French (19%) Italian (8%)
Nationality	*noun:* Swiss *adjective:* Swiss
Currency	Swiss Franc (CHF)
Primary Religions	Catholic (46%) Protestant (40%)
Population	7,450,000
Capital / Population	Zurich / 972,000
Other Large Cities / Population	Geneva / 179,000 Basel / 163,000 Lausanne / 117,000

DRIVING FACTS

License	Minimum driving age is 18. A valid driver license must be accompanied with your passport.
Speed Limits **(If not posted)**	Built up areas — 50 kph / 31 mph Major roads outside towns — 80 kph / 50 mph Highways — 120 kph / 74 mph
Speed / Distance	Kilometers Per Hour KPH / Meters – Kilometers
Side of the Road	Drive on the right side of the road unless One-Way
Roundabouts	Vehicles in the roundabout have the right-of-way over vehicles entering the circle. When in the roundabout, drive in a COUNTER-CLOCKWISE direction.
Seat Belts	Front Seats — Required Rear Seats — Required if available Children — • Under 12 years and less are not allowed in front seat unless in an approved child restraint device
Traffic Lights	The rules governing traffic lights are the same as in the U.S.
Right on Red	No, unless green arrow is present.

Required Equipment	Warning triangle
	First aid kit
	Extra bulb kits and fire extinguishers are recommended.
Pedestrians	Pedestrians and bicyclists have an unconditional right-of-way over vehicles turning left or right. Right-of-way in crosswalks is determined by local signage.
Tolls	Drivers on the Autobahn (expressway) must display a "vignette" pass in the windshield. They can be purchased at the border crossing points or service stations before entering the country.
Parking	The Blue Zone system applies. Discs may be purchased from gas stations, garages and police stations.

Fuel	Unleaded Super 95 octane	*Vleifrei /sans Plomb / sensa Piomba*
	Diesel	*Diesel*

Motorcycles	Helmets are mandatory
	Headlights required at all times
Fines	Law enforcement may collect fines during the traffic stop. Be sure to get an official receipt.

Drinking and Driving	You will be considered to be impaired and subject to arrest if your BAC is .08% (.8 mg.ml) or more.
U.S. State Department Traffic Safety and Road Conditions	Safety of Public Transportation: Excellent Urban Road Conditions/Maintenance: Excellent Rural Road Conditions/Maintenance: Excellent Availability of Roadside Assistance: Excellent

EMERGENCY TELEPHONE NUMBERS

Police	117
Fire	118
Ambulance	117 or 114
US Embassy	Jubilaumsstrasse 93 CH-3005 Bern Tel: 031-357-7011 Fax: 031-357-7344

TERMS OR WORDS YOU MAY SEE ON THE ROAD

> **(Depending on the region, see Germany, France or Italy for applicable translations)**

An excuse you might try if involved in a traffic accident. (According to urban legends, it worked in the U.S.)

Ich hatte einen Zusammenstoss mit einem stillstehenden LKW.

(German Translation: "I collided with a stationary truck coming the other way.")

A great opening line for that awkward moment you absolutely cannot think of a way to start a conversation.

Si une poupée Barbie avait une taille humaine, elle mesurerait 95-60-90, et sa hauteur serait de 2 mètres 18.

(French Translation: "If the American Barbie doll were life-size, her measurements would be 39-23-33 inches. She would stand seven feet, two inches tall.")

28 TURKEY

LOCAL SPELLING: *TÜRKIYE*
ABBREVIATION: TR

Much of Turkey's interior terrain is similar to the Rocky Mountains coupled with nearly 2,000 miles of shoreline on the Black Sea in the North and the Mediterranean Sea on the South Border. Western Turkey is rich with religious history, most notably Selçuk and Ephesus where you will find the burial place of St. John the Evangelist and encounter the Temple of Hadrian and the 24,000-seat Great Amphitheater (which until recently was still used for open-air concerts).

One of the nicer surprises of Turkey is the Black Sea coast, where Jason and the Argonauts sought the Golden Fleece. Seldom crowded, the drive will offer spectacular beauty, and great culinary opportunities. The terrain along the Black Sea is relatively flat. For contrast, the shoreline along the southern coastline offers windy roads sandwiched between the mountains to the north and cliffs overlooking the beautiful Mediterranean Sea. Antalya is the number one tourist destination for the Turks on vacation. Should you desire a totally different driving experience, southeastern Turkey may be your calling. It is the northern extension of the Syrian plain - translation: hot and flat and best visited in the winter. Central Turkey offers the "Silk Road" and other trade routes thousands of years old, which pass amazing terrain features and Persian architecture of every type.

Any time you drive out of the built up areas, fill your gas tank at every opportunity as the quality of gas in the rural areas can be problematic; and, do not count on your credit cards being accepted at many gas stations. Turkey is another one of those countries that made those old defensive driving lectures so valuable. Turkish drivers routinely ignore traffic laws including driving through red lights and stop signs and turning left from the far right hand lane; official turning lanes are a rarity in Turkey. Be sure you purchase full insurance coverage, because out of country insurance companies will most probably not cover incidents occurring in Turkey.

Turkey shares many of the same issues as Greece when one is considering driving to Turkey from other countries. Careful attention to your car rental agreement is crucial to ensure you do not unknowingly drive into countries prohibited by your contract or local laws. Here too, your best bet may be to arrive by plane/ boat/train, and rent your car in Turkey.

It comes as no big surprise that terrorists are somewhat more active in the eastern countries. While Turkey is certainly much safer and more progressive than many of the Muslim countries, one would be well advised to check with the Department of State's *Travel Warnings* and *Public Announcements*, and register with the local Embassy.

FAST FACTS

Area	480,580 Sq. Kilometers or 185,552 Sq. Miles Slightly larger than Texas
Primary Language	Turkish
Nationality	*noun:* Turks *adjective:* Turkish
Currency	Turkish lira (TRL)
Primary Religions	Muslim
Population	68,900,000
Capital / Population	Ankura / 3,500,000
Other Large Cities / Population	Istanbul / 10,050,000 Izmir / 2,220,000 Bursa / 1,289,000 Adana / 1,220,000

DRIVING FACTS

License	Minimum driving age is 18. A valid driver license must be accompanied with your passport.	
Speed Limits **(If not posted)**	Built up areas	50 kph / 31 mph
	Major roads outside towns	90 kph / 56 mph
	Highways	120 kph / 74 mph
Speed / Distance	Kilometers Per Hour KPH / Meters – Kilometers	
Side of the Road	Drive on the right side of the road unless One-Way	
Roundabouts	Vehicles in the roundabout have the right-of-way over vehicles entering the circle. When in the roundabout, drive in a COUNTER-CLOCKWISE direction.	
Seat Belts	Front Seats	Required if installed in the vehicle
	Rear Seats	Recommended
	Children	Children under 12 years of age are not allowed in the front seats
Traffic Lights	The rules governing traffic lights are the same as in the U.S.	
Right on Red	No, unless green arrow is present.	

Required Equipment	Warning triangle
	First aid kit
	Tow rope
	Tool kit
Pedestrians	Pedestrians and bicyclists have an unconditional right-of-way over vehicles turning left or right. Right-of-way in crosswalks is determined by local signage.
Tolls	Tolls are charged on several of the main highways
Parking	Watch for signs: *Park Yapilmaz* means No Parking. Do not park within 25 meters of danger signs.
Fuel	Unleaded Super 95 octane	*Kurşunsuz Benzin*
	Diesel	*Dızel*
Motorcycles	Helmets are mandatory
Fines	Law enforcement may collect fines during the traffic stop. Be sure to get an official receipt.

Drinking and Driving	You will be considered to be impaired and subject to arrest if your BAC is .05% (.5 mg.ml) or more.
U.S. State Department Traffic Safety and Road Conditions	Safety of Public Transportation: Fair Urban Road Conditions/Maintenance: Fair Rural Road Conditions/Maintenance: Fair Availability of Roadside Assistance: Fair

EMERGENCY TELEPHONE NUMBERS

Police	155
Fire	110
Ambulance	112
US Embassy	110 Ataturk Blvd. Kavaklidere, 06100 Ankara Phone: (90-312) 455-5555 Fax: (90-312) 467-0019

TERMS OR WORDS YOU MAY SEE ON THE ROAD

English	Turkish
Attention	Dikkat
Bed and Breakfast	Oda ve Kahvaltı
Caution	Dikkat
Car	Araba
Car Rental Agency	Kiralık Araba Sirketi
Diesel	Dizel
East	Doğu
Entrance	Giriş
Exit (roadway)	Çıkış
Expressway	Ekspres Yol
Forbidden	Yasak
Gasoline	Benzin
Hospital	Hastane
Hotel	Otel
Left (direction)	Sol
Motor Oil	Motor Yağı
Museum	Müze
No Parking	Park Yasak
North	Kuzey
One-way	Tek Yön
Parking	Otopark
Parking Lot	Otopark
Passenger Vehicle	Yolcu Araci
Police	Polis
Police Station	Polis Karakolu
Restaurant	Restoran
Right (direction)	Sa ğ
Road Closed	Yol Kapalı
Room for Rent	Kiralık Oda
Slow	Yavaş
South	G üney
Street	Cadde
Toll Road	Paralı Geçiş
Truck	Kamyon
Welcome	Hosgeldin
West	Batı
Yield	Yolver

An excuse you might try if involved in a traffic accident. (According to urban legends, it worked in the U.S.)

Kazanin asıl sebebi küçük bir arabadaki koca ağızılı küçük bir adamdı.

(Translation: "The indirect cause of this accident was a little guy in a small car with a big mouth.")

A great opening line for that awkward moment you absolutely cannot think of a way to start a conversation.

Akvaryum balığın karanlık bir adada bekletirseniz, sonunda beyazlaşacaktır.

(Translation: "If you keep a Goldfish in the dark room, it will eventually turn white.")

Translation courtesy of Orkun Alatas

UNITED KINGDOM

LOCAL SPELLING: *UNITED KINGDOM*
ABBREVIATION: UK

Other than driving on the ~~wrong~~ left hand side of the road, the American tourist planning a driving vacation will find the United Kingdom very easy to acclimate to (See the chapter titled "On The Left."). But first a little history lesson. The United Kingdom consists of England, Wales, Scotland and Northern Ireland. (Ireland is its own country and the people are very proud of their independence.) Rule #1, How to get along with the locals: Never, ever, call a Welsh, Scots or Irishman, "English." Welsh is a very distinctive language, as are the Irish and Scottish Gaelic languages, but English is the predominant language and all traffic signs are written in the Kings English. With the exception of a few idioms, most U.S. citizens can easily communicate anywhere within the UK.

There has been a history of unrest in Belfast which is fairly well contained to a small area. Safety should not be a big concern if you will just give Belfast a wide berth.

The UK offers some of the best driving opportunities possible (hence the birth of the term "British Touring Car"). Across the southern portion of the island are lightly traveled, well-maintained roads that will take you to Stonehenge and through the New Forest where you may catch a glimpse of wild ponies. A little north and you are at Shakespeare's home in Stratford-upon-Avon, not far from the Iron Bridge in Shropshire County, reputed to be the seed of the industrial revolution. You may also get a glimpse of Roman ruins and take a hot sauna in original Roman built spas in the town of Bath. The drive westward into Wales offers opportunities to visit several castles, some still occupied and some in ruins. You may even find castles that have been converted into hotels and Bed and Breakfasts. Don't be surprised when you find yourself driving on a single-laned road through Wales (see "priority signs" in the Road Sign chapter). A more northerly drive will take along the paths traveled by Robin Hood in the Sherwood Forest, and the land of King Arthur; and, on to Scotland to look for the elusive Loch Nes Monster. The golfing enthusiast may reserve a tee time at the world's most famous golf course, St. Andrews; a little expensive, but certainly doable. Any trip to Scotland during the summer months would not be complete without a visit to one of the Highland Games which take place along the route from Aberfeldy to Tomintoul. Regardless where your destination may be, your drive will be along picturesque roads lined with rock walls, through far reaching meadows, scenic mountains, past farms and quaint villages that are hundreds of years old, and along majestic seascapes along the English Channel and the North, Irish and Celtic Seas.

Drive to the west coast town of Stranraer and you can catch a ferry to Northern Ireland and a whole new list of traveling experiences. The ferry ride is about two and one-half hours.

London is not a car friendly environment. In fact, a £5 daily "Congestion Charge" is required if you wish to drive in Central London between 7 a.m. and 6:30 p.m., Monday through Friday. And, once you get there, you will find parking extremely expensive. Of all my travels, I found Oxford to be the absolute worst town I have ever driven in. One would think that with all the brilliant minds housed in that city, a better traffic plan could be put to use; but take heed, when the sign at the bus stop on the edge of town recommends "Park and Ride," park and ride! Because you may not wish to miss many of the attractions in the larger cities, make plans to use public transportation. They have been doing it for a long time and the buses, subways and trains are easily navigated.

FAST FACTS

Area	244,820 Sq. Kilometers or 94,925 Sq. Miles Slightly smaller than Oregon
Primary Language	English, Welsh (26%), Scottish form of Gaelic
Nationality	*noun:* British, Brions, Brits *adjective:* British
Currency	Pound sterling £ (GBP)
Primary Religions	Anglican and Roman Catholic (66%)
Population	60,271,000
Capital / Population	London / 11,219,000
Other Large Cities / Population	Glasgow / 1,100,000 Birmingham / 972,000 Liverpool / 462,000 Edinburgh / 460,000

Author's Note: An excellent book to read while driving southern England is *Stonehenge*. This historic fiction mixes the relics found throughout southern England with the lives of mythical characters. Artifacts found at the actual Stonehenge site, coupled with those in the Salisbury Museum tie the past and future together before your very eyes.

DRIVING FACTS

License	Minimum driving age is 17.	
	A valid driver license must be accompanied with your passport.	
Speed Limits *(If not posted)*	Built up areas	50 kph / 31 mph
	Major roads outside towns	100 kph / 62 mph
	Highways	130 kph / 80 mph
Speed / Distance	Miles Hour MPH / Miles	
Side of the Road	Drive on the LEFT side of the road unless One-Way	
Roundabouts	The U.K. is all about roundabouts! You might even find double-rotaries, what a skater calls a figure-8; and rumor has it there are even a couple triples. Vehicles in the roundabout have the right-of-way over vehicles entering the circle. If driving on the other side of the road doesn't test your skills enough, the Brits' roundabouts also circle backwards. Don't forget, when entering a roundabout in the U.K., be sure to drive in a CLOCKWISE direction.	
Seat Belts	Front Seats	Required
	Rear Seats	Required if available
	Children	• Children under 3 years are not allowed in the front seat unless in an approved seat or harness.
		• Under 3-12 but under 1.5 meters must use an appropriate child restraint adult belt.
Traffic Lights	As in the U.S., Green means GO and Red means STOP. Amber signals to STOP until the intersection is cleared of traffic. You may then proceed safely. Red+Amber signal means PREPARE TO GO.	

Right on Red	No, unless green arrow is present.
Required Equipment	Warning triangle and first aid kit are recommended.
Pedestrians	Pedestrians and bicyclists have an unconditional right-of-way over vehicles turning left or right. Right-of-way in crosswalks is determined by local signage.
Tolls	There are no tolls on the expressways or "carriageways." Some bridges and tunnels do require tolls.
Parking	Pay-and-display parking is common throughout the country. Watch carefully for parking instructional signs before leaving your car parked. A receipt may be obtained from a nearby kiosk and must be visible through the windshield. Red lines or double yellow lines mean No Parking. The large zig-zag lines were not painted by a drunk street striper, the also mean No Parking as do rows of road studs. "When all spaces are full, simply place your car at the front of any chosen car actually parked legally, rev the bloody guts from your engine and drop the clutch. Moments later, once the smoke has cleared and the smell of burning tyres subsided, you have a parking space. Now casually leave your car, obtain a parking token and go shopping!!!" *Created from an actual event as told by Constable Bill Williams, Romsey, England.*

Fuel	Unleaded Super 95 octane	*Petrol* (which is usually advertised in terms of imperial gallons - 1.19 US gallons per Imperial Gallon. Of course in true British fashion, the pumps most often measure in liters.)
	Diesel	*Diesel*

Motorcycles	Helmets are mandatory Headlights required at all times
Fines	There are standard fines in the UK, payable to the magistrate, similar to the way we do it in the US.
Drinking and Driving	You will be considered to be impaired and subject to arrest if your BAC is .08% (.8 mg.ml) or more.
Misc.	It is illegal to use a cell phone while driving.
U.S. State Department Traffic Safety and Road Conditions	Safety of Public Transportation: Excellent Urban Road Conditions/Maintenance: Excellent Rural Road Conditions/Maintenance: Excellent Availability of Roadside Assistance: Excellent

EMERGENCY TELEPHONE NUMBERS

Police	999
Fire	999
Ambulance	999
US Embassy	24 Grosvenor Square London, W1A 1AE Tel: [44] (0)20 7499-9000

THE LANGUAGES OF THE UNITED KINGDOM

The United Kingdom is a country of many cultures and languages. Most prominent are Scottish, Welsh, Irish, and what the British call English.

English, the primary language of the United Kingdom, will be found on all traffic signs, regardless of where you are; however, when you drive through Scotland, Wales and Northern Ireland, you will find that the road signs are in both English and the local language.

In the following pages, translations have been provided, not to fill a need of a prospective foreign driver, but simply as a matter of interest and education.

ARE THEY REALLY SPEAKING ENGLISH?

Normally, this section is dedicated to translations needed to navigate through a specific country. In the United Kingdom, this is of little consequence. The signs are easily read. There are, however, some words that do not translate so easily across the sea.

American	British
Battery	Accumulator
Car Fender	Wing or bumper
Car Hood	Bonnet
Car Trunk	Boot
Convertible Top	Hood or Soft Top
Dashboard	Fascia
Gallon	Equals 1.25 US Gallons
Gas	Petrol
Glove Box	Cubby Box
Horn	Hooter
Large truck	Juggernaut
Muffler	Silencer
Oil Pan	Sump
Tire	Tyre
Tractor-trailer	Articulated lorry or Artic
Trailer	Caravan or motor home
Truck	Lorry
Windshield	Windscreen

Terms Or Words You May See On The Road

American	British
Breakdown lane	Lay-by
Divided highway	Dual Carriageway
Exit	Junction
Highway	Motorway
Overpass	Flyover
Parking Lot	Car Park
Rotary	Roundabout
Subway	Underground or Tube
Traffic jam	Tail back
Yield	Giveway

Words That Might Get You In Trouble

American	British
ATM	Hole-in-the-wall
Cigarette	Fag
Condom	Johnny
Elevator	Lift
Erasure	Rubber
Flashlight	Torch
French Fries	Chips
Gum	Glue
Jello	Jelly
Jelly	Jam
Lawyer	Solicitor
Outlet	Power point
Potatoe Chips	Crisps
Sausage	Banger
School Crossing Guard	Lollipop lady
Slot Machine	Fruit Machine
Sweater	Jumper
Tic-Tac-Toe	Naughts and Crosses

TERMS OR WORDS YOU MAY SEE ON THE ROAD

English	Welsh	Scots Gaelic
Attention	Dalier sylw	Aire
Bed and breakfast	Gwely a brecwast	Leabaidh agus bracaist
Caution	Rhybudd	Faiceall
Car	Car	Càr
Car rental agency	Asiantaeth rhentu car	Buidheann Charaichean Mhàl
Detour	Gwyriad	Bealach
Diesel	Dîsl	Dìosail
East	Dwyrain	Ear
Entrance	Mynedfa	A-steach
Exit	Allanfa	A-mach
Expressway	Gwibffordd	Rathad-mhòr (rathad)
Forbidden	Gwaharddedig	Toirmisgte
Gasoline	Petrol	Gas
Hospital	Ysbyty	Ospadal
Hotel	Gwesty	Taigh-òsda
Left	Chwith	An taobh chlì
Motor oil	Olew modur	Ola Motair
Museum	Amgueddfa	Taigh-tasgaidh
No parking	Dim parcio	Chaneil Pàirceadh
North	Gogledd	Tuath
One-way	Unffordd	Aon-slighe
Parking	Parcio	Pairceadh
Parking lot	Maes parcio	Pàirc Charaichean
Passenger vehicle	Cerbyd cario pobl	Carbad Neach-siubhal
Police	Heddlu	Poileas
Police Station	Gorsaf Heddlu	Stèisean Poileas
Restaurant	Bwyty	Aite-bìdh
Right	Dde	An taobh dheas
Road closed	Ffordd ar gau	Rathad Duinte
Room for rent	Ystafell i'w rhentu	Rùm airson Màl
Slow	Araf	Slaodach
South	De	Deas
Street	Stryd	Sràid
Toll road	Ffordd toll	Rathad Chìs
Truck	Lori	Truca
Welcome	Croeso	Fàilte
West	Gorllewin	Iar
Yield	Ildiwch	Gèill

An excuse you might try if involved in a traffic accident.

BRITISH ENGLISH:

On the way to the hole-in-the-wall I was reaching for a fag and I didn't see the solicitor step in my way. I bopped my hooter just before he struck my wing.

(Translation: "On the way to the ATM, I was getting a cigarette and did not see the lawyer in the street. I honked my horn, just before he (the lawyer) struck my fender.")

WELSH:

Roedd y polyn ffôn yn agosau'n gyflym. Roeddwn yn ceisio ei osgoi pan darodd blaen fy nghar.

(Translation: "The telephone pole was approaching rapidly. I was attempting to swerve out of its way when it struck the front end of my car.")

A great opening line for that awkward moment you absolutely cannot think of a way to start a conversation.

BRITISH ENGLISH:

The bird over the jump with the bone got nice railings in the boat race.

(Translation: "The girl on the phone behind the bar has nice teeth.")

WELSH:

Chwefror 1865 yw'r unig fis mewn hanes nad oedd ynddo leuad llawn.

(Translation: "February 1865 is the only month in recorded history that did not have a full moon.")

Word variations provided with the assistance of Bill Willaims and Rich Adams
Welsh translation courtesy of D. Rhys Prytherch
Scotts-Gaelic translation courtesy of Helen Eddie

SECTION III
APPENDIXES

APPENDIX A
WEIGHTS AND MEASURES CONVERSIONS

SPEED AND DISTANCE CONVERSION

The figures in this table apply to both speed and distance.

Miles	Kilometers		Kilometers	Miles
MPH	KPH		KPH	MPH
5	8.0		5	3.1
10	16.1		10	6.2
15	24.1		15	9.3
20	32.2		20	12.4
25	40.2		25	15.5
30	48.3		30	18.6
35	56.3		35	21.7
40	64.4		40	24.9
45	72.4		45	28.0
50	80.5		50	31.1
55	88.5		55	34.2
60	96.6		60	37.3
65	104.6		65	40.4
70	112.7		70	43.5
75	120.7		75	46.6
80	128.7		80	49.7
85	136.8		85	52.8
90	144.8		90	55.9
95	152.9		95	59.0
100	160.9		100	62.1
			105	65.2
			110	68.4
			115	71.5
			120	74.6
			125	77.7
			130	80.8

To Convert KPH to MPH - (KPH)*0.621=MPH
To Convert MPH to KPH - (MPH)*1.609=KPH

TEMPERATURE CONVERSION

Celsius	Fahrenheit		Fahrenheit	Celsius
-20	-4		-20	-29
-10	14		-10	-23
0	32		0	-18
10	50		10	-12
20	68		20	-7
30	86		30	-1
36.6	98.6		40	4
40	104		50	10
50	122		60	16
60	140		70	21
70	158		80	27
80	176		90	32
90	194		98.6	36.6
100	212		100	38
110	230		110	43

FORMULAS
$F=(C*1.8)+32$ $C=(F-32)*.55$

Note: For the mathematical purist: .55 = 5/9 and 1.8 = 9/5

LIQUID MEASURE

Liter	US Gallon	UK Gallon
1	0.3	0.2
5	1.3	1.1
10	2.6	2.2
15	4.0	3.3
20	5.3	4.4
25	6.6	5.5
30	7.9	6.6
35	9.2	7.7
40	10.6	8.8
45	11.9	9.9
50	13.2	11.0

FORMULAS
L x .3 = US Gal L x .2 = UK Gal UKG x 1.2 = US Gal   USG x .8 = UK Gal

APPENDIX B

TOURIST SEASON CHARTING WORKSHEET

By doing a little detective work and using the charts below, you can determine the best time to take your vacation. Remember, High and Low Seasons are often separated by a couple days. As you narrow your time bracket, be sure to check a couple days either way; especially in the beginning and end of the summer season and around the Christmas holidays. Remember too, it is more expensive to fly on weekends than on weekdays.

EXAMPLE	Date	Day	Date	Day	Date	Day	Date	Day
Depart	3/5	Sat	3/3	Thu	6/4	Sat	6/2	Thu
Return	3/19	Sat	3/18	Thu	6/18	Sat	6/16	Thu
Airfare	$ 655		$ 612		$ 912		$ 741	
Hotel	$ 89	/day	$ 89	/day	$ 110	/day	$ 110	/day
Auto	$ 40	/day	$ 40	/day	$ 55	/day	$ 55	/day

	Date	Day	Date	Day	Date	Day	Date	Day
Depart								
Return								
Airfare	$		$		$		$	
Hotel	$	/day	$	/day	$	/day	$	/day
Auto	$	/day	$	/day	$	/day	$	/day

	Date	Day	Date	Day	Date	Day	Date	Day
Depart								
Return								
Airfare	$		$		$		$	
Hotel	$	/day	$	/day	$	/day	$	/day
Auto	$	/day	$	/day	$	/day	$	/day

You are welcome to copy this page and use it as a worksheet to plan your vacation.

APPENDIX C
INTERNATIONAL TELEPHONE CALLS

IDD (INTERNATIONAL DIRECT DIALING) is the international prefix needed to dial a call FROM the country listed TO another country. The IDD numbers may change and some countries have more than one IDD.

COUNTRY CODE - The country code is the national prefix to be used to dial TO one country FROM another country. You may also need to dial a city or area code. When a country name appears in the table as a link, there will be additional information regarding city or area codes.

NDD (NATIONAL DIRECT DIALING) is the number used to make a call WITHIN a country from one city to another. In the U.S. we use 1. As in the U.S., this number may not be necessary for local calls.

Examples (Calling from/to)	IDD	Country Code	NDD	Area Code	Telephone Number
Vienna, Austria Orlando, FL, USA	011	43		1	987 65 4
Orlando, FL, USA Vienna, Austria	00	1		407	987-6543
Innsbruck, Austria Vienna, Austria			0	463	987 65 4

Country	IDD	Country Code	NDD
Austria	00	43	0
Belgium	00	32	0
Czech Republic	00	420	n/a
Denmark	00	45	n/a
Finland	00, 990 994, 999	358	0
France	00 (France Telecom) 40 (TELE 2) 50 (OMNICOM) 70 (LE 7 CEGETEL) 90 (TELECOM)	33	0
Germany	00	49	0
Greece	00	30	n/a
Hungary	00	36	06
Ireland	00	353	0
Italy	00	39	0
Liechtenstein	00	723	n/a
Luxemburg	00	352	n/a
North Ireland	048	353	0
Norway	00	47	n/a
Poland	00	48	0
Portugal	00	351	n/a
Scotland *	00	44	0
Spain	00	34	**
Sweden	00	46	0
Switzerland	00	41	0
Turkey	00	90	0
United Kingdom	00	44	0
United States of America	011	1	1

* Same as U.K.

**In 1998 Spain enacted a new dialing system. All area codes begin with 9. All telephone calls must include the area code and number, including cell phone calls.

D APPENDIX D
ROAD SIGNS

MORE THAN YOU PROBABLY WANTED TO KNOW:
Most of the traffic signs In the European Union are standardized following the 1968 Vienna Convention, with some changes introduced in 1971 and 1973.

The vast majority of the road signs in Europe are self-explanatory. There are, however, some subtle differences such as the pedestrian silhouette in a red triangle as opposed to in a red circle. In general, red circles mean NO or PROHIBITED. Red triangles typically mean CAUTION or DANGER.

THE BASICS

RIGHT-OF-WAY

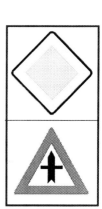

The narrow roads and constricted driving areas have forced the Europeans to adopt a systematic system of ensuring all drivers understand who has the right-of-way or priority. Priority roads are marked with a yellow diamond with white border. Most notably, road signs will picture thicker and thinner roads. The thicker roads have the right-of-way and drivers on the thinner roads must yield. Review carefully the following section labeled, "Priority Signs" for other types of right-of-way signs you will encounter.

PROHIBITED VS. CAUTION

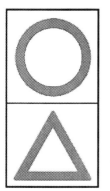

The **RED CIRCLE** indicates
1. Road Closed
2. Speed Limit Sign
3. No, Prohibited: the prohibited action will be identified by an image within the circle.

Do not look for the red diagonal line used in the U.S. with the red circle.

The **RED TRIANGLE** indicates a condition requiring caution. The image within the triangle will identify the type of possible hazard.

DIAGONAL LINES

 Diagonal lines on signs in Europe characteristically mean the end of something such as leaving a town, or the end of a speed zone.

SPEED RESTRICTION SIGNS

In the EU, you will find two types of speed regulatory signs: 1) Speed Limit; and 2) Recommended Speed. Speed Limit means specifically what it says. While there is no speed limit on many of the primary highways in Germany, you will see Recommended Speed signs. That places the responsibility of your actions on you. You will also find Recommended Speed signs in congested areas, roads that have extreme conditions such as tight curves, extreme weather changes, etc.

Speed Limit	End of Speed Limit	Electronic Panel Speed Limit	Recommended Speed	End of Recommended Speed

PRIORITY SIGNS

The U.S. translation for "Priority" is *Right-Of-Way*. Seldom if ever seen in the U.S., European Priority Signs are some of the most common, most important and least understood by American Drivers. Many roads in Europe are very narrow and allow little room for vehicles to pass. Understanding the Priority Signs provides order in an otherwise chaotic situation.

STOP	Priority Road You have the right-of-way	End of Priority Road You no longer have the right-of-way	Yield to Oncoming Traffic	Your lane has the right-of way

Yield to main road ahead	Intersection ahead, with single road on the left, you have the right-of-way	Intersection ahead, with single road on the right, you have the right-of-way	Intersection Ahead, your road has the right-of-way	Access Allowed Two way traffic, neither lane has priority

One-Way Road	One-Way Road

PASSING SIGNS

No Passing	End of No Passing Zone	Trucks not allowed to pass	End of Truck No Passing Zone

RAILROAD SIGNS

Single Track Railroad Crossing	Multiple Track Railroad Crossing	Railroad Crossing With Gates Ahead	Railroad Crossing Without Gates Ahead	Tram Crossing

PARKING SIGNS

CAUTION - DANGER SIGNS

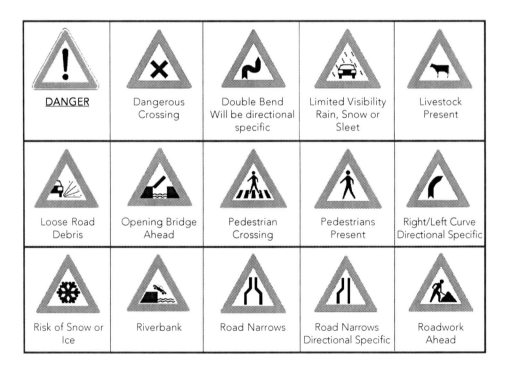

Roundabout	School Crossing	Slippery Road	Steep Hill Downhill	Bicycle Riders Present
Traffic Signal Ahead	Two Way Traffic	Uneven Road	Wild Animals	

INSTRUCTIONAL SIGNS

Built Up Area	End of Built Up Area	Drive Either Way	Drive Ahead Only	End of Restrictions (Electronic Sign)
End of Restrictions	Go in Direction	Go in Directions	Go in Directions	Keep Right/Left (Direction Specific)
Main Roadway	End of Main Roadway	No U-Turns	Roundabout	

LIMITED ACCESS SIGNS

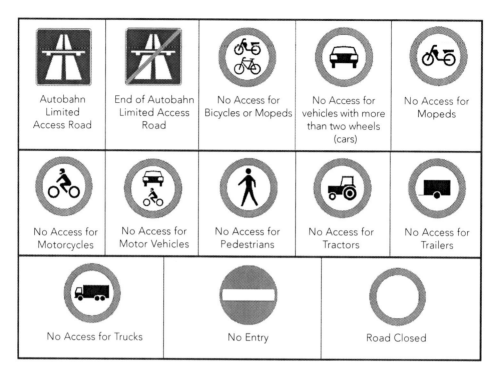

HEIGHT AND WEIGHT SIGNS

Although these signs will probably never apply to an American Tourist, they will answer the never-ending question, "What the heck does that mean?"

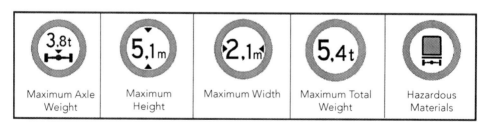

ACCOMMODATION SIGNS

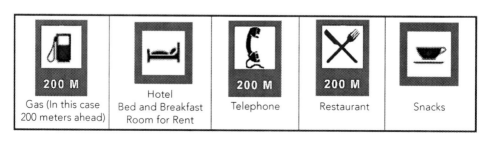

Printed in the United States
79480LV00006B/153

9 781599 754895